Washington Gladden

The Christian League of Connecticut

Washington Gladden

The Christian League of Connecticut

ISBN/EAN: 9783743321878

Manufactured in Europe, USA, Canada, Australia, Japa

Cover: Foto ©Lupo / pixelio.de

Manufactured and distributed by brebook publishing software (www.brebook.com)

Washington Gladden

The Christian League of Connecticut

THE CHRISTIAN LEAGUE

OF CONNECTICUT

BY

WASHINGTON GLADDEN

THE CENTURY CO.
NEW-YORK

THE CHRISTIAN LEAGUE OF CONNECTICUT.

I.

THE first of the many snow-storms that made memorable the winter of eighteen hundred and seventy-five had just fallen on the smooth roads of New Albion; a slight thaw with a following frost had polished up the sleighing, and two hearty-looking gentlemen, behind a powerful gray horse that needed no urging, were taking their first taste of the winter pastime. They seemed to be enjoying it; for, as they flew past the pedestrians toiling along the sidewalk, their faces shone and their laughter rang merrily. The one who held the reins was a man of forty, smooth-shaven, but for a narrow, brown side-whisker; with a clear and fair skin, into which the stinging winter air was bringing a healthy crimson tint; a strong chin, a well chiseled nose and brow, a blue eye, and a kindly smile. You would have guessed he was a clergyman, and would have missed; he was the cashier and manager of the First National Bank of New

Albion. The other was perhaps a little younger, with dark skin, full beard, and bright, black eye; his figure was slight but well made, and he wore a gray ulster, and a sealskin cap without a visor; a journalist, you would have said, or perhaps an artist, and would have been wrong again; for he was the Rev. Theodore Strong, pastor of the Second Congregational Church in the same thriving town. The cashier, Mr. Franklin, was his parishioner, and had been his college classmate; the old friendship had been the cause of the minister's location in his present pastorate, and was now one of its strong supports. Old Major, the good gray horse, had learned well the way to the parsonage, before which he used often to halt after banking hours; whence the parson, if he was to be had, was whirled away for a breezy hour or two on the country roads. These drives with his old friend were unadulterated recreation. It was a distinct understanding between them that the cares of the bank and the parish were always to be left behind.

"No shop, now, old fellow!" Franklin had said when he came for his friend the first time; "religion and business ought to be mixed sometimes, no doubt; but, for you and me, just now, rest is both business and religion."

To such a respite the hard-worked parson was nothing loth, and the hours thus spent were full of the keenest delight. All anxieties being resolutely left behind, the minds of both friends were free to take in every fresh phase of roadside beauty, every new glory of sky or river or meadow. Other common pleasures they had in books and studies beyond the range of their work, of which they communed with much invigorating conversation; while, as each was a good story-teller and sure to pick up a budget of mirthful anecdote, their discourse was plentifully spiced with fun.

It must not be inferred that the banker always refused to consult with the pastor about the parish work; on the contrary, he was his most trusted and judicious counselor; it was only that these hours of recreation were sacredly guarded from the intrusion of professional anxieties.

On this December afternoon the talk had ranged widely as usual, and had kept clear, as usual, of all work-day topics, when, suddenly, Mr. Strong, in a tone half apologetic, broke out:

"'Ware, Walt! I'm coming perilously near to the Second Parish in my next remark—as near as Bradford."

"Twenty miles! Rather dangerous! Well, go ahead; but see that you keep your distance."

"The matter is this: Johns, of the East Church, in that metropolis, is trying to start a

Congregational club, into which he wants to gather all of that ilk in this region,— representatives, at any rate, of all the principal churches; he has written me to come up to help him incubate the project. Shall I go?"

"Yes, go, and 'sit on it' hard."

"You are explicit, as usual. Now tell me why. Don't you like Congregational clubs?"

"Never tried one. But clubs are generally wooden things. What is it proposed to do with this one?"

"Oh, there is to be a supper, of course, once a month; and a paper read by somebody after supper, and a discussion of the paper, and a general powwow after the discussion."

"Just so. Stuff, talk,— that's a club. But what special topics do you think this one will be most apt to light on?"

"Denominational topics, largely, of course; how to consolidate our churches; how to increase the *esprit du corps;* how to promote our various benevolent enterprises."

"Certainly. It is part of a movement to stiffen the last syllable of that sesquipedalian sectarian substantive, 'Congregational*ism*.' I do not like the name at all, and the sting in its tail, which it is now proposed to sharpen and harden, is the part I like least."

"There you go again," laughed the parson. "It's a downright insult, Major, when a man with such a horse as you are insists on riding a hobby."

"Oh, well," continued the banker, "there's nothing particularly sinful in this indulgence that the Bradford Congregationalists propose; doubtless, the fellows who like to run things will enjoy it much, but I doubt if the outcome is valuable. There will be some increase of good-fellowship, and much burning of incense under the nose of the idol of the tribe. The more perfect the success of the club shall be, the further off will be the practical coöperation to which we must come at last."

"There is truth in what you say," answered the parson; "and I own that I am coming more and more to your way of thinking about such matters. But when two ride a hobby one must ride behind, and I am not yet quite so fierce a foe of the sects as you are."

For a few moments there was silence, broken only by the click of Major's hoofs upon the icy road and the sough of the wind through the pine forest by the side of which they were driving.

"Look here, Theo," the banker at length continued, " couldn't we do a better thing?"

"Several things, no doubt. But what, for instance?"

"Couldn't we organize a Christian League Club here in New Albion?"

"Softly, softly, sir; you are breaking over bounds."

"I know I am; but you began it."

"And what was said, a few minutes ago, about clubs?"

"I remember; but there are clubs and clubs. This need not be a wooden one—indeed, it couldn't be; it would have to be made on a very pliable pattern."

"Show us how."

"The thing has no shape in my own mind yet; but why shouldn't we strike for a little practical Christian union in this town? We have enough of the sentimental sort, and bad enough it is. The union meetings of the week of prayer always bring out the prayer-meeting rounders,—men who have no standing in their own churches nor among their fellow-citizens; men like old Bill Snodgrass, who can reel off cant by the fathom, and whose word, in any business transaction, is as good as his bond only because neither of them is worth a row of pins. There never is a union meeting in which Bill doesn't exalt his horn at least twice. Then there is young Cyrus Smiley, the effusive and irrepressible, and Tom Trafton, the censorious sputterer, whose prayers are mainly digs at the ministers."

"I know it," broke in Mr. Strong, greatly amused at the vivid characterization of his friend. "But have you heard Trafton's last on his own pastor?"

"No; what was it?"

"Dr. Sampson told me the story himself. You know that Tom has taken a special dislike to the Doctor, and betrays it in all his prayers. The other night, in the prayer-meeting, he said, in his jerky way: 'O Lord, grant that our temp'r'l food may not be so skerse and poor as the spiritooal food pervided for us; for ef it is, we sh'll all be in the poor-house within six months.'"

Franklin laughed.

"Tom outdid himself that time. Think of letting such a creature loose in a prayer-meeting! But that is the sort of person that revels in union meetings. At home he can be suppressed, at least in part; but a joint service of the churches gives him vent. So that, practically, our attempt at Christian union consists mainly in meeting together a few times a year, to be rasped and disgusted by these persons who put themselves forward as the representatives of our common Protestantism. Now, I wonder whether some plan could not be devised by which the real people in our churches could be brought into working union, and the flood-trash kept out."

"Yes, that's the question. But you don't seem to get ahead very fast in answering it."

"Patience, patience, young man! We'll work

this thing out, but it will take time. The fact is, New Albion is an excellent place to start such an experiment. The relations between the churches are amicable; there has been no unnecessary multiplication of religious societies as yet; there are no churches here that ought to be killed, except one or two colored churches; the population is intelligent, the ministers are all good friends; the thing can be done."

"Undoubtedly, my eloquent friend; but what thing?"

"We can have a meeting, from time to time, of the ministers and certain representative men of the various churches, to consult about the interests of morality and religion in this community. That's the dry bones of it."

"The next question is how to make these dry bones live."

"Yes, and you must help me solve that. Your practical tact and skill in managing people come in play just here."

"Thank you! I wish devoutly that something of the sort could be brought about, and I will do my best to devise a feasible way of accomplishing it. But it must be managed cautiously. Don't flush your game!"

Old Major had arrived at the parsonage, and the parson dismounted, with a promise to give the matter of which they had been talking early and full attention.

II.

THE problem which we have seen the banker and the parson getting ready to attack is a knotty and an urgent one. How to bring the Christian churches of our country into practical unity; this is a question round about which a great deal of talk has been going on, but to the careful consideration of which but few minds have been turned. All the discussion has vibrated between two points: the desirableness of a spiritual fellowship among denominations, and the feasibility of an organic union of the denominations. A great multitude agree in saying that the sects ought to dwell together in unity,—that is to say, that the ministers ought to exchange pulpits, and that members ought to pass freely by letter from one church to another, and that Christians ought to meet now and then in union meetings, and say pleasant things in their prayers and speeches about one another, and sing together

"Blest be the tie that binds,"

and so on. So much of Christian union as this, nearly everybody believes in. The more strenuous sectarians stick at some of these points, but not very persistently; to refuse this much involves some measure of opprobrium. But there are many who insist that, while Christian union may have this extent, it can have no more; that it is vain, and, indeed, rather sacrilegious to ask for anything beyond this. Others declare that this sentimental union is of no value; that what we want and must have is organic union, a consolidation of all the sects into one church, so that Protestantism shall stand over against Romanism, compact and united, all under one central government, moving with well ordered and harmonious march to the conquest of the world. These two conceptions have divided between them the debaters about Christian unity; and it must be owned that each side brings against the other arguments that are well-nigh unanswerable. The believers in what is called spiritual unity insist that the organic unity asked for is impossible; the believers in organic unity declare that spiritual unity, as it now exists, is of very little consequence.

Some abatement of these extreme views must, indeed, be made on both sides. The measure of unity to which the churches have already attained is by no means to be despised; their relations are vastly better than they were forty years ago, when Presbyterians or Congregationalists had no more dealings with Methodists or Baptists than the Jews once had with the Samaritans; when keen contempt and bitter abuse were common currency among the sects. It is not a slight, but an important gain, that Christians of all names are able now to meet together on friendly terms in social worship. On the other side, it is too much to say that the dream of the Church existing as one compact body can never be realized. Stranger things than that have come to pass. The truth lies about midway between these disputants. The spiritual unity to which we have attained, though not worthless, is ridiculously inadequate to the present need of the Church; and the organic unity for which we are exhorted to labor, though it may not be impossible, is yet a long way off. Is there not, somewhere between the emotional fellowship of the present and the organized ecclesiasticism of the future, a measure of coöperation that is both desirable and attainable? This was the problem to which the practical mind of Mr. Walter Franklin had turned. He was a man, as his pastor well knew, who had a way of bringing things to pass; and Mr. Strong was not therefore surprised, at the close of the next Sunday evening's service, to be joined at the church door by his friend, with an ominous gleam of speculation in his eyes.

"Pretty well used up to-night, Theo?" he queried. The Romans knew how to convey more delicately the hope of a negative answer.

"Not at all," said the minister, who never knew on Sunday night how tired he was. "Fresh as a lark. Come home with me, and we'll have it out."

"Have what out?"

"That matter that you're eager to talk about. You have done bravely in keeping away till the Sunday work was over, and I haven't the heart to put you off any longer. Come on."

"Seems to me I have detected a few delicate allusions to it in sermons and prayers to-day. Your mind's as full of it as mine is, dissembler! And I'm only going over with you to find out your plans."

"Well," said the parson, as he let his friend in at the door of the parsonage, "it has been on my mind now and then, I own. And the place to begin is Jerusalem. I saw Dr. Phelps last week, and, in talking about church sociables and so forth, I asked him why the Old Church did not sometimes invite their neighbors to their festivities. He took me up at once, of course, and told me very cordially to come over to their sociable on Tuesday evening, and to bring along

a good delegation of the Second Church people.
I replied that it was rather hard to be obliged to
beg an invitation; but that I should pocket my
humiliation and go, which seemed to please the
old gentleman mightily. So I want you and
your wife, and Deacon Hunter and his wife, and
Shaw and his mother, and the Burnham girls,
and a few others — a dozen or fifteen of our
wide-awake people — to meet here on Tuesday
night, and we will go over in a body and take
'em by storm."

"Capital!" exclaimed Franklin. "The church
sociable is one of the strongholds of sectarian
exclusiveness; if we can capture that and turn
its guns upon the enemy, one great point will
be gained."

"There is no need of despising the church
sociable," replied the minister. "It serves a
good purpose, and is no more accountable than
the Church itself for 'sectarian exclusiveness.'
Human nature is to blame for that, not the
Church, nor the sociable."

"But I am not talking about remote causes,"
persisted the banker. "What I see is this: the
church sociables in most of our villages and large
towns cut up society into cliques. Active and
zealous church members find but little time for
the cultivation of social relations beyond the
bounds of their own parishes. I have heard it

said, more than once, by intelligent citizens, that there is not much general social intercourse among the best people of this town, and that the fault lies at the doors of the churches. The First Church people are a set by themselves, and so are the Second Church people, and the Episcopalians, and the Baptists, and all the rest. The devotion of the church members to their own societies hinders the development of a broad, social life."

"That is true," answered Strong, "and there is something here to regret, beyond question. Nevertheless, there are compensations, which you, Walter Franklin, must not overlook. If the churches have somewhat hindered the cultivated classes outside of the large cities from consorting together, they have also helped to bring together the cultivated and the uncultivated classes, and that is one of the things that most need to be done. They have substituted vertical lines of division in society for horizontal ones. Bad as the church cliques are, they are not so bad as the stratifications of social æstheticism. But I am not defending social exclusiveness in the churches; I am trying to overcome it, as a step toward something higher."

"You are perfectly right, and you may count on me. We will be on hand Tuesday evening. Good-night!"

It was a merry company that followed Mr. Strong into the parlors of the First Church; and though they were received at first with polite bewilderment, it was not long before hospitality and good-fellowship asserted themselves in the heartiest fashion. The hosts exerted themselves to entertain their guests, voted the innovation a delightful one, and promised to return the visit. This was the beginning of a series of fraternizations among the churches of New Albion; none were neglected; the Adventists, who worshiped in Central Hall, and the two colored churches, were surprised in their turn by visiting delegations from the other churches that dropped in at their prayer-meetings, and stopped afterward to shake hands and to say a few pleasant words. So far as it could be done socially, the ecclesiastical *entente cordiale* was fairly established in this prosperous town.

All this was so much of the nature of a recreation, that the banker and his friend excepted it from the list of forbidden subjects, and often chanted the praises of Christian fraternity to the music of Major's sleigh-bells.

"It is all excellent, so far as it goes," said the banker, one day in January; "but I want to see the thing put on a business basis. The improvement in the social relations of the churches is a great gain; it signifies vastly more to have the people meet in this friendly way, and show each other neighborly courtesies, than to have them talk the cant of Christian union now and then in a prayer-meeting—but it is not enough. We want some method by which this fraternity shall have a distinct and influential expression."

"Exactly," answered the parson; "we have been getting up steam; now we want to utilize our power. How shall we do it?"

"I thought you were managing the business," replied Franklin; "but, since you ask the question, I'll give you my idea. Let us have a little party at my house some evening, including the ministers and about three of the best members of each church, and see what comes of it."

"How shall the three best members of each church be chosen?"

"We must choose them ourselves. We know this community well enough to pick our men."

The preparation of this list was not, however, an easy matter, as the banker and his pastor found. Mr. Franklin's knowledge of the business standing of the "leading members" served to thin out Mr. Strong's ample catalogue of nominees.

"Rodney Merrill? Yes; he's a good talker, but his word doesn't stand for much. Better put young Porter, the carpenter, in his place. Stevenson? H'm! He's a customer of mine; but I don't like his way of doing business.

Montgomery? I've got some memoranda on Montgomery. He failed not long ago; and not ten days before the collapse he borrowed a thousand dollars at our bank, solemnly assuring me that he had not less than twenty thousand dollars in available assets, and not more than five thousand dollars of debts. The inventory showed that his figures were exactly right, only the debts were twenty thousand, and the assets five. It was a mere slip of the tongue, no doubt; but we'll pass Montgomery. This company must be a clean one, and there is no lack of sound and reputable men in our churches."

"How about the colored brethren?" queried Mr. Strong.

"The colored brethren must be left out," was the answer; "not for social, but for ecclesiastical reasons. One of the first duties of this league of ours, if it ever gets into operation, will be the suppression of these colored churches. When the colored people abandon their own organizations, and join the other churches, they may come in as representatives from them. We will have no color-line in the Christianity for which this club stands. I'll go as far as any other man in fraternizing with colored men; but with colored churches, never. The sectarianism whose only basis is the color of the skin is the meanest kind of sectarianism."

III.

OUT of the thirty-two persons invited, thirty, representing all of the eight churches of New Albion, gathered in Mr. Franklin's parlors on the sixteenth of January. The clergymen were all present, and the absentees were not conspicuous. Tea was served in the parlors, and Mr. Franklin was amused to see how completely sectarian lines were blotted out in the grouping of the guests about the small tables. To the eye of the social devotee it would have seemed, no doubt, a mixed multitude—people of all grades of society were here; but the hospitality was so frank and hearty, and the entertainment of such a simple sort, that the humblest people were at their ease. And what was of more consequence, these people were all known to one another as being engaged in various kinds of benevolent work in the community; the *cameraderie* of Christian service was a stronger bond than that by which most social circles are drawn together. Dr. Emmons Hopkins Phelps, the venerable and well beloved pastor of the " First Church of Christ in New Albion," was *tête-à-tête* with the Rev. Murray Henderson, the young pastor of the Universalists; Dr. Thomas Sampson, the stalwart wit and excellent scholar, who adorned the pulpit of the Baptist Church, was cheek by jowl with the genial Dr. Philip Strickland, of St. Mark's Episcopal Church; and here and there Congregational deacons were sandwiched between Episcopal vestrymen and Methodist stewards.

"What are you going to do with your happy family when you get them trained?" asked the Rev. John Wesley Thorpe, Methodist, of the beaming host.

"Travel with 'em," was the prompt answer. "Take 'em up to Hardscrabble and West Northfield, and over to Hockset, and show 'em to the natives for ten cents admission, the proceeds to be divided equally among the home missionary societies of the several denominations."

"Such a show would be a great curiosity in those parts, no doubt," said the clergyman. "But my friend Peters, here, thinks that the saints in Hardscrabble would be horrified to see Dr. Phelps eating and drinking with a Universalist."

"It is somewhat bewildering, I own," replied the banker. "But I think that, when they looked into Henderson's face, they could say nothing against it. Look at him now! It's a face for Raphael."

"Solar radiance, isn't it?" responded Peters. "And the man is as saintly as he looks. His church is growing in all the graces a great deal faster than mine is. I wish the Free Baptists had half as good a minister."

"What do you imagine that your bishop would do, if he were to look in upon this company?" asked Dr. Sampson of Dr. Strickland.

"I imagine," was the answer, "that he would go straight to Dr. Buck, the editor of your "Inquisitor," and tell him all about it."

"Very likely," laughed the Baptist. "And probably the two would sit down and have a pleasant chat over it. Each one would try to make out that the people of his communion were a little nearer ready for fellowship than those of the other."

"Oh, of course! But I should like to know what Franklin has got in his head. He has not invited this carefully selected company for merely social purposes, you may depend. He means business."

"Well," answered Dr. Sampson, glancing about the room, "he will not be able to carry this company into any very wild scheme. It is a pretty solid set of men, Dr. Strickland—about as good as New Albion contains, that's a fact. A set of men," the Doctor went on, after a pause, "who, if they should put their heads and hands together, could give the old Adversary a great deal of trouble."

The company was not left long in doubt as to the plans of the host. Half an hour after supper, Mr. Franklin rose, and there was silence.

"I have called you together this evening, gentlemen," he said, "to consult about a matter of importance. The unity of feeling now existing among the religious societies of this town is gratifying, and it has occurred to me that out of it something might grow that should be for the permanent good of the community. We have learned to treat each other courteously in social intercourse; can we not work together? The Christian work of this town is imperfectly done, because what is everybody's business is nobody's. The churchless classes are not reached; the poor are neglected; pauperism thrives upon our careless and indiscriminate charity. Could we not, by meeting occasionally for consultation about this work, secure a much more thorough performance of it? There is much flagrant vice in our streets; hundreds of our young people are being led into temptation and destroyed. Could we not, by combining our efforts, secure a more vigorous enforcement of the laws for the suppression of vice, and set on foot some effective movement for the rescue and reclamation of these young men and women? Furthermore, the good feeling now existing among us is likely to be disturbed at no distant day. The town is growing rapidly; other religious organizations will be needed; strife may arise among the denominations for the occupancy of new fields. Is it not possible for a band of Christian men, representing all the churches, to exert an influence which shall lead to the amicable adjustment of all such questions? I am sure that there is not a man in this company who would not at once put the interests of religion and morality in this community above the interests of the sect to which he belongs. If this is true, then we can, if we choose, make it the rule in New Albion that all Christian work shall be prosecuted, not on the worldly principle of competition, but on the Christian principle of coöperation. Is not this worth attempting? In order to bring the matter to a point at once, I will read you a draft of a plan of operation prepared by my friend, Dr. Strong, and myself."

"CONSTITUTION.

"1. This organization shall be known as The Christian League Club of New Albion. It shall consist of the minister and three laymen from each of the following churches of this town: Adventist, Baptist, First and Second Congregational, Free Baptist, Methodist Episcopal, Protestant Episcopal, and Universalist. Delegations from other churches hereafter formed may be admitted by unanimous consent.

"2. The object of this organization shall be to hold stated meetings for consultation respecting the Christian work to be done in New Albion and its suburbs, and the best methods of accomplishing this work. The visitation and evangelization of the churchless classes, the distribution of Bibles and of good literature, the establishment of new missions when needed, the care of the poor, the prevention of vice and crime by the enforcement of the laws, the opening of coffee-rooms, reading-rooms, and other safe places of resort, the furnishing of cheap and wholesome diversion for the young — these subjects and such as these will be matter of consultation at the meetings of this club.

"3. The members of this club shall never be required to assent to any creed or confession of faith, nor shall doctrinal or theological discussions of any kind ever be allowed in its meetings. The club shall assume no authority over its members or over the churches, and, to guard against any such encroachments, it shall never vote on any question. Committees may be appointed by the chairman, at any meeting, to carry out the views of the club; but no such committee shall be appointed without unanimous consent of the members of the club.

"4. Meetings shall be held on the first Monday evening of every month, at the houses of the members, by invitation. The member at whose house the meeting is held shall preside. No records shall be kept, and the club shall have no permanent officers.

"5. When a vacancy occurs in the lay delegation of any church, it shall be filled on nomination by the pastors of *the other* churches, who shall constitute a committee for that purpose. No pastor shall have any voice in the nomination of delegates from his own church, and no name shall be reported by the committee of pastors on which they are not unanimous. If no objection is made to the name thus reported, the nominee shall be notified of his election.

"This sketch of a plan of organization," continued Mr. Franklin, as he folded the paper, "brings before you, as distinctly as I am able to do it, the thought in my own mind. I will not make any further remarks about it. I hope that, in the free conversation that may follow, the wisdom of the scheme will be freely canvassed, and its defects, if defects there be, will be pointed out."

The company had listened with an absorbed and rather anxious attention to the banker's speech. At its close, the only response was a rather ostentatious sigh of relief by Dr. Strickland, whereupon the whole assembly broke out laughing.

"Not quite so bad as you feared, eh?" said Dr. Sampson.

"N-no," replied the other, meditatively; "I don't yet see how such an institution could do any particular mischief."

"Its hands would be so effectually tied," said Mr. Thorpe, "that it could do no mischief; but are they not so effectually tied that it could not do much good?"

"How so?" asked Mr. Strong.

"Well, the provisions about voting and keeping records, for instance; I don't see how an association forbidden to vote can effect much."

"But we do not vote in prayer-meetings or sociables," responded Mr. Strong; "are not they of some service? Would not frank and frequent conferences about the state of religion and morals in this town be instructive and stimulating, even if we took no votes?"

"Perhaps so," answered the Methodist pastor.

"The truth is," said Dr. Sampson, with much energy, "that this voting business is more often a snare than a help in all sorts of organizations. A vote is simply an expression of will, and the tendency to put will in the place of reason and love is the bane of all ecclesiasticism."

"But you believe in the rule of the majority, do you not?" queried Deacon Squires, of the First Church.

"No, I don't. I submit to it because it is practically the best thing to do, and sometimes the only thing that can be done. But the principle that the majority shall *rule* implies a division of sentiment that ought always, in religious work, to be avoided if possible. The less we have in our Christian assemblies of ruling and of being ruled the better."

"The minority ought to be expected to coöperate," suggested Mr. Peters.

"Certainly," answered Dr. Sampson, "and they ought to coöperate. But if half the energy that is expended in voting people down were expended in conciliating and persuading them, we should have fewer church quarrels and fewer disaffected and sullen minorities. It is a favorite superstition of this age that nothing can be done without a vote, whereas very little that is of permanent value is ever done by voting."

"It is clear," said Dr. Phelps, quietly, "that such a body of men as this would be must jealously guard itself against the assumption of ecclesiastical power. Perhaps the denial of a vote is none too stringent a safeguard against this danger."

"Well, I don't object to it," answered Mr. Thorpe. I can see that such a club might do some good work without voting, and it would surely avoid some dangers."

" But why not let the minister have some voice in selecting the delegates from his own church?" asked the Baptist Deacon Jones.

"That," answered Mr. Franklin, "simply relieves the minister of a delicate responsibility, in the exercise of which he might cause disaffection in his own church."

" But why not let the church choose its own representatives?" asked Elder Bates of the Adventists.

" Because," answered Mr. Strong, " that would give to this body an official and representative character, which we do not wish to have it possess.

By and by the churches of this city may be ready to delegate to a body representing them some supervisory powers; they are not yet ready to do any such thing, and we want nothing, therefore, that looks like it."

"I have a little misgiving," suggested Mr. Henderson, "as to the wisdom of a select and exclusive organization like this. Why not have an open meeting once a month for such purposes — a meeting called from all the pulpits, and open to all?"

"Don't!" cried Dr. Sampson, amid the laughter of the company. "The cranks and blatherskites of all the churches would be there in force, and the knowledge that they would be there would keep all the sensible folks away."

"I surrender!" said the Universalist pastor, good-naturedly. "You know, brethren, that my experience in union meetings is somewhat limited."

"Well," said the Methodist minister, after a short pause, "the plan seems to meet with general favor, and in order to test the sense of this meeting, I move you, sir,—— no, I beg pardon — I take it all back; go ahead, Mr. Franklin."

And the parson sat down, laughing with the rest at his own blunder.

"The shape in which the matter lies," said the banker, "is just this: Here are the pastors of the eight churches named in the constitution, and three laymen from each of them, with one vacancy in the lay delegation from the Baptist Church, and one from the Episcopal Church. I propose that, if there is no objection, the persons here present constitute The Christian League Club of New Albion. There will be two vacancies, and these may be filled according to the constitution. I will wait a few moments for objections."

No voices were heard, and Mr. Franklin proceeded: "The consent is complete, and we may regard the club as organized. It is, gentlemen, a most gratifying result. What will be accomplished we will not venture to predict; but I have faith enough in the common sense and Christian spirit of this body of men to believe that they can talk frankly and earnestly about Christian work in this town without getting into any disputes, and that they will be ready to put the interests of virtue and religion above their private preferences or their sectarian prejudices. If such a temper and purpose shall rule in all our meetings, I am sure that public opinion will be wisely directed, and that substantial results will follow."

All formalities were now at an end, and promiscuous conversation followed. Mr. Franklin was too wise to introduce any questions for discussion at this meeting; he preferred to let the members of the club work up their own questions.

The talk that ensued was full of suggestions; these energetic, clear-headed business men took hold of the problem put into their hands with the grip of their trained faculty, and it did not take them long to find out that the business of doing good in their community had been carried on in a negligent, perverse, and wasteful fashion, and that there was plenty of room for the introduction of better methods. One thing and another were spoken of as possible and desirable, by the various groups that were exercising their wits upon the problem, and difference of opinion began to be developed at once; but these differences engendered no heat. The need of perfect good nature was evident, at once, to all who had any points to carry. Inasmuch as nothing could be done in this club without unanimous consent, it would never do to irritate anybody. Fair consideration, and entire recognition of the right of others to hold contrary opinions, must be the basis of all these conferences. This was a warfare in which nothing but sweet reasonableness could win.

At ten o'clock the company dispersed, having accepted Dr. Sampson's invitation to hold the next meeting at his house, on the first Monday evening in February.

IV.

HOW to reach and help the churchless classes was the question that received the most attention in the free talk of the members of the Christian League Club at their first meeting; the topic had been upon the minds of many of them during the interval, and it was sure to be prominent among the themes of the second conference.

"It is plain," said Deacon Squires, after the company had settled down to business in the cozy parlors of Doctor Sampson, "that there are large numbers of persons in this community wholly outside of all religious influences. Those who attend our churches every Sunday constitute a small part of our population. Sunday before last was a beautiful winter's day, and the congregations were, as I have been told, unusually large in all the churches. On that day, to satisfy myself, I had a careful count made of all the congregations, and here are the figures. I will not read them, but the total number of persons present on that Sunday morning was two thousand seven hundred and sixty-nine. Out of a population of twelve thousand, this is not a good showing. Something must be done, or we shall lapse into heathenism."

"That showing," replied the chairman, "is rather discouraging on the face of it; but let us see if it will not look better after a little examination. Out of the twelve thousand people living in this town, at least three thousand are Roman Catholics. The great majority of these attend church. This leaves nine thousand to divide among the Protestant churches. Will Deacon Squires kindly tell us how many there were in the congregation at the Baptist Church, Sunday before last? I do not care to number my neighbors, but I am willing to have my own flock counted."

"Five hundred and seventy-six," answered the Deacon.

"That is about what I had supposed," said the chairman. "Now, our Sunday-school in the afternoon numbers fully four hundred, and at least half of these were not at the morning service. At the evening meeting I am sure that we often have at least a hundred who have not attended either of the other services. During that Sunday we must, therefore, have had in our church nearly nine hundred different persons belonging to our parish, besides strangers and sojourners. You would need to add fifty, and, I think, in many cases, sixty per cent. to the morning congregation, to get the number of persons reached by the churches on any given Sunday."

"And that," said Mr. Franklin, "would bring the figures up to between four and five thousand actually present in our Protestant churches on a pleasant Sunday."

"Yes, that is about what I calculated — nearly half of all the Protestants in town get to church at least once on a fair day."

"But that," said Deacon Jones, is not a good story to tell. More than half of all the Protestants in town *stay away* from church every fair Sunday. Put it that way, and how does it sound?"

"But that," continued Dr. Sampson, "needs further explanation. A large share of all these Protestants are unable to attend church on any given Sunday. Add together all the children under four years old, the aged and infirm, the sick, and all those who must stay at home to attend upon these, and you will have, according to some careful English estimates, about forty per cent. of the population. Suppose, now, that forty-five per cent. of the people actually attend church, and that forty per cent. are providentially kept away: you have not more than fifteen per cent. of the population who are, both by choice and by habit, neglecters; and the careful canvass that our church has made of a section of the town that is fairly representative of the whole, leads me to the same conclusion. I do not believe that more than fifteen or twenty per cent. of our people can be counted among those who are outside of all the churches. I happen to know, for example, how many souls are in my parish. I have tried to get the names of all, old and young, who are under my pastoral care— all the members of all the households connected with my church and Sunday-school, and not connected with any other church, and the list numbers about fourteen hundred names. Many of these are persons who do not often attend Sunday service—they are semi-attached parishioners; but if you should ask them where they go to church, they would mention the Baptist Church. They consider me their pastor, and would send for me if they needed the services of a clergyman. So that the actual members of my parish who are cared for, in some sort, by my church, number considerably more than twice as many as my congregation number on a pleasant Sunday morning. If this is true of all the other churches, and it undoubtedly is, then there must be in the neighborhood of seven thousand persons connected more or less closely with our Protestant parishes. At the outside, I do not think there can be more than two thousand persons in this town who are not, in some imperfect way, cared for by our churches, either Catholic or Protestant."

"That puts a different face upon the question," said Deacon Squires, "and I am glad to have the subject so carefully analyzed. But two thousand heathen are too many."

"Most true," cried Dr. Sampson, "and it is a shame to our churches that there are so many. It is well to have distinct ideas of the work we are trying to do, and not to exaggerate its magnitude, lest we be discouraged. This whole subject has been greatly obscured by a number of shallow alarmists, who have been croaking about the desertion of the churches, and who have wholly failed to comprehend the real facts. But if the real facts are not half so black as they have been painted, they are somber enough, and it is high time that we were grappling with the problem they present."

"What to do about it is the question," said Mr. Franklin.

"Why not send for an evangelist?" modestly queried Elder Bates, of the Advent Church. "Brother Moody is not to be had this winter; but we might get Brother Weeks. He is said to be a powerful preacher—abler even than Moody;

and he might succeed in drawing in some of these neglecters."

"Drawing them into what?" asked Mr. Franklin.

"Why, into his meetings. I suppose that they would be held in the Town Hall, and many would be drawn in who do not attend the churches."

"Doubtless; and they would attend the churches no more after Mr. Weeks had gone away than they did before. A few would join the churches, but the proclamation thus made of the inadequacy of the churches to supply the religious wants of the community would do these outsiders, as a class, an amount of harm for which these small gains would poorly compensate. Building a fire in the Town Hall is a poor way of warming the churches."

Mr. Franklin spoke very quietly, but with the earnestness of strong conviction, and the only response was a fervent "Amen" from Dr. Phelps. It was plain that the project was not popular, and good Elder Bates forebore to press it.

"Couldn't we do something with mission Sunday-schools?" suggested one of the Methodist laymen.

"Where would you put them?" asked Mr. Strong.

"Oh, I don't know; good places might be found, I should think."

"Down on the corner of King and Patterson streets is a good location," said Mr. Thorpe.

"That is about fifty rods from the Free Baptist Church," answered Mr. Strong. "Do you want any help down that way, Peters?"

"I fear," said the genial parson, "that we are not doing all the work we ought to do; but there is still a little room left in our vestry for new scholars."

"Beg your pardon, Peters," cried the Methodist. "I didn't intend to poach on your preserves; I was only thinking of doing good on general principles."

"We must be careful to make our general principles fit the special cases with which we have to deal," said Dr. Sampson.

"I am unable," said Mr. Strong, "to think of any neighborhood in which a mission school could be started that is not now within reach of some existing church. Around the new brassworks now building, in the south part of the town, a settlement is likely to spring up that will soon need to be provided for; at present, every locality is well furnished with churches."

"But," said Deacon Squires, "people will often attend mission chapels who would not attend churches."

"The first thing to do in such a case," replied Mr. Strong, with emphasis, "is to convert or kill the churches of which this is true. A church into which poor people cannot be induced to go ought to be born again or blotted out. The church whose methods of administration and whose social atmosphere are such as to discourage the attendance of the poor, is driving Christ from its door. Is not this His own word, 'Inasmuch as ye did it unto one of the least of these, ye did it unto me?' It is entirely possible to create and maintain in our churches a spirit and a way of working that shall make the poorest people feel perfectly at home in them. The church in which these are not found needs a missionary as much as the Patagonians do. It has not yet learned the alphabet of Christianity."

"You wax warm, Brother Strong," cried Dr. Sampson. "Haven't you got a missionary or two up at the Second Church that you can send to some of your neighbors?"

"Not one. We need them all," answered the parson, laughing. "But I suspect that I have already scattered abroad a few, to whom my doctrine on this subject was too hot, and who have gone forth preaching quite another gospel. Whatever help you can get out of them you are welcome to. Good riddance to them, I say. One or two of them have taken refuge with you, Strickland. I hope you will convert them."

"I'll do my best to convert them, at any rate," said the rector, warmly. "If they expected to hear a softer doctrine on this subject at St. Mark's, they have probably found out their mistake by this time. Our practice is not quite up to our theories; but I am happy to say that the spirit of a genuine Christian democracy is growing among our ecclesiastical aristocrats. The churches are not few in which the poor are coddled or patronized; those in which they are respected and frankly put upon the same level of consideration and responsibility with the rich and well-to-do are not yet a multitude. This is our standard, and, although we have not reached it, we shall not lower it, please God, under the present administration."

"This discourse is edifying," said Mr. Peters. "Go right on, brethren. It is good to hear such testimony from the pastors of such churches."

"We sometimes hear of 'a saying hard to shape in act,'" said Dr. Phelps, "and this is one of them. The theory is sound; but whenever thought is wedded to fact there will be a bridal dawn of grumbling, if nothing worse, in some of our congregations."

"The more shame to us," cried Mr. Strong, "if we have suffered our people to forget the true function of the Christian Church, and have allowed the fellowship of the Spirit to degenerate into a chartered snobbery."

"But," said Mr. Thorpe, "is it not wiser to recognize existing facts and adapt our methods to them? It is certainly a fact that the poor people generally think they are not wanted in the churches. They greatly exaggerate this inhospitality; in many of our churches they would find a cordial welcome; but they think that the place where the rich and the stylish people worship is not the place for them. Many of those who stay away from the churches could be gathered into mission chapels. Is it not better to reach them in this way than fail altogether to reach them?"

"I think not," was the answer. "The one injurious and fatal fact of our present church work is the barrier between the churches and the poorest classes. The first thing for us to do is to demolish this barrier. The impression is abroad among the poor that they are not wanted in the churches. This impression is either correct or incorrect. If it is correct, then there is no missionary work, for us who are pastors, half so urgent as the conversion of our congregations to Christianity. If it is incorrect, we are still guilty before God in that we have allowed such an impression to go abroad; and we are bound to address ourselves, at once and with all diligence, to the business of convincing the poor people that they are wanted, and will be made welcome, in the churches. But every mission chapel planted in the neighborhood of a church, and intended for the poor, is an ostentatious proclamation to the poor that they are right in their impression; that we freely consent to the separation of the rich from the poor in worship; that we approve of the religion that is founded upon caste. To that proclamation I will never put my signature. The time has come when judgment should begin at the house of God, and when the paganism that masquerades in our stylish churches, in the guise of Christianity, should be stripped of its disguises and banished from our altars."

Mr. Strong had risen from his seat, and his black eyes were blazing with the intensity of his convictions, as he finished his speech. A round of applause greeted his peroration. It was clear that no progress could be made by the club in the erection of mission chapels until some population not accessible to the churches could be found.

"Well, gentlemen," said the genial chairman, "the question is before you. What will you do for the churchless classes,—be they few or many, rich or poor?"

"Would it not be wise," asked Mr. Henderson, "to have the town divided into geographical districts, as many as there are churches, each of which should be assigned to a church for its special field? It would not be possible to have each church stand in the center of its field, for some of our churches are too near neighbors; but we might come as near to that as possible. If every part of the town was thus under the care of some church responsible for its evangelization, our work would be well begun. Each church could do the work in its own district in its own way."

"That is a sensible suggestion," said Mr. Franklin. "I move"——

"Order!" cried the Methodist parson. "'Physician, heal thyself!'"

"Peccavi!" exclaimed the banker. "The forensic habit survives, as you see, in the millennium of the Christian League. But we have one resource. A committee can be appointed by unanimous consent. I trust that such consent will be given to the appointment by our chairman of a committee of three, who shall carefully divide the town into districts, assigning one to each church; and that this committee may report at the next meeting."

To this proposition no objection was made, and the chairman at once named as the committee Mr. Franklin, Mr. Henderson, and Deacon Squires.

The work of the committee was done before the next meeting. The population of New Albion was distributed, as it is in most similar towns, in such a way that it was possible, in the words of Deacon Squires, to give each church "a streak of lean and a streak of fat,"—to assign to each a district in which there were sections inhabited by the poor, as well as those inhabited by the well-to-do. When the assignment was made, it was at once reported by the pastors to the churches. The knowledge that a systematic and concerted effort was to be made to reach all classes in the community stimulated each church to do its own part of the work promptly and thoroughly. So it came about that, before the winter was over, the whole town had been covered by the canvassers, and no household was left in ignorance of the fact that a place and a welcome were waiting for it in one of the churches.

Some of the canvassers carried with them cards, on which were printed the hours of their various services. The spirit of good-will and coöperation was such that the visitors generally sought to gratify the denominational preferences of those on whom they called. If a Congregational visitor found a family with Baptist proclivities, he sent the address of this family to the nearest Baptist visitor. In this way the poor people obtained a strong impression of the unity of the churches. It became evident that this enterprise was not undertaken for the aggrandizement of any sect or of any local church, but rather for the sake of carrying the gospel greeting and invitation to all the destitute. Many cases of sickness and want were also discovered by the visitors, and the practical charities of the churches began to be developed in an effective way. A colporteur of the Bible Society appeared upon the scene as the work was beginning, himself proposing to canvass the town in the interest of his society; but he was easily persuaded to relinquish the work into the hands of the local visitors.

"Well," said the parson to the banker, as they drove slowly along a forest road, on a bright May afternoon, drinking in the aromatic breath of the newly opened leaves, "the weather has considerably moderated since that day, last January, when we were passing this spot, and when you suggested the formation of our club."

"Yes, and I think the ecclesiastical climate has softened a little."

"Not a little. The outcome has been wonderful. The results are far greater than I ever dreamed of. There is really a great deal of good-will among men, if it can only get a chance to express itself."

"We will give it plenty of chances. This work is only fairly begun. There is abundance of work to do better than any we yet have done. And we shall do it. The Christians of New Albion have got a taste of the luxury of Christian coöperation, and they will never go back to the beggarly elements of a selfish ecclesiasticism."

V.

BEFORE the end of the summer vacation, the brass-works at New Albion were in operation, and a large colony of mechanics had occupied the tenement houses of the "Patch" above the mill. For the use of this new community, the town had provided a school-house; a neat hall above the company's store gave room for religious services. The mill was a mile and a half from the nearest church, and something must be done to supply the religious wants of the new community. The question arose at the September meeting of the Christian League Club.

"What is to be done for the brass-workers?" asked Mr. Strong.

"I believe," answered Mr. Thorpe, blushing a little, "that our people have already taken steps toward organizing a church in that neighborhood."

"Indeed!" exclaimed Dr. Sampson. "The Baptists have also consulted me about services there, but I declined to express any opinion until some conference had been held upon the matter by this club."

"I want it understood," answered Mr. Thorpe, "that I have done nothing about it. One of the overseers at the mill is a zealous Methodist, and he has found out that quite a number of the hands belong to our connection. The presiding elder was down there the other day, and conferred with him about it. But I felt as the Doctor did, that it would hardly be right for me to help in the enterprise until we had talked it over here."

"Would it not be well," asked Mr. Strong, "to call a public meeting in the hall at the brass-works, of all persons who desire the organization of a religious society, and let them determine for themselves what kind of an organization they will have?"

"That is fair," was the verdict of several voices.

"Let us have a committee of seven,—one from each of the denominations represented in this club,—who shall call this preliminary meeting, and be present to take charge of its deliberations."

This was the suggestion of Mr. Peters.

"Good!" was the general response.

"And now," said Mr. Franklin, "I hope nobody will object to my proposition, which is that this committee consist of the pastors of these churches, omitting the pastor of the Second Church. The Congregationalists should not outnumber the others on the committee; and I am sure that the presence of these seven pastors at a meeting of this character will be to the brass-workers an impressive object-lesson in Christian unity."

"Mr. Franklin is exactly right," said Mr. Strong. "My absence will not be misinterpreted, and Dr. Phelps is competent to represent the Congregationalists."

The proposition was therefore unanimously agreed to, and a handbill, signed with the names of the seven pastors, called the people of the brass-works together on the next Sunday afternoon. The hall was filled with an interested company. Dr. Phelps, as the senior pastor, took the chair.

"We have called you together," he said in his brief opening speech, "because we assumed that there must be, among the six or seven hundred people of this new settlement, a large number who would desire some sort of religious organization, and because we, the pastors of the Protestant churches in New Albion, desired to assist you if we could in forming one. I know that I speak for all of my brethren when I say that none of us cares so much to have a church of his own particular sort formed here, as to have the people here happy in their church relations. We have learned, in New Albion, to dwell together in unity, and we want you to live in the same way. Whatever kind of church is formed here, if it be only a church that owns and follows Jesus Christ, it will receive the right hand of fellowship from every one of our churches. It is evident that there ought not to be more than one church in this small community; we have come to assist you in deciding what form that organization shall take. I understand that some steps have been taken toward forming a Methodist church here. We shall have no objection whatever if the society takes that form, if that is the wish of the community; we only care that you should be heartily agreed among yourselves, and work together harmoniously."

Three or four of the other pastors followed with short speeches, each of whom testified, with equal clearness, to the desire of all for unity and coöperation among the Christians at the brass-works.

"And now," said Dr. Phelps, "we propose to submit this matter to the decision of those interested. Those who wish to have a religious society organized in this place, and who will pledge themselves to assist in supporting it, either by contributions, by Christian work, or by attendance upon its services, will please rise."

About fifty men and women stood up.

"Very good! Now, for convenience, will those who have thus pledged themselves occupy the seats in the right-hand corner of the hall."

The audience, like most audiences, was a little reluctant to make this change of seats, but it was at length accomplished, and the corner was occupied by a respectable-looking company, of which one-third were men.

"We shall now," said Dr. Phelps, "distribute among you slips of paper, on which you are requested to write the name of the denomination in accordance with whose rules you wish this society to be organized. If you want a Methodist church, write 'Methodist'; express your preference on your ballots."

"If you please, sir," said a stout, ruddy-faced young Englishman, standing up in the right-hand corner, "I have just come over from the old country, and I know but little about your churches here; in England I went to chapel; but I like what I have heard this afternoon, and I wish that the new church might be the same kind that these gentlemen belongs to that has come down here to help us organize, if you will tell me the name of it."

There was a little laugh; but the Englishman was unaware of his blunder, and he kept the floor, waiting to be answered.

"What gentlemen do you refer to?" asked the Doctor, blandly.

"The seven gentlemen on the platform," was the answer.

"The church to which we all belong," replied Dr. Phelps, soberly, "is the Church of Christ."

"Thank you, sir," said the Englishman, taking his seat; "I vote for the Church of Christ."

To some of the thorough-going denominationalists this seemed a good joke; but the Englishman's positive decision served for wisdom to several of the uninstructed, while many others, perceiving the difficulty of agreeing upon any existing sect, took the cue and wrote his vote upon their ballots. When the slips were collected, there were ten Methodist ballots, six Baptist, three Congregational, one Episcopalian, one Presbyterian, one Lutheran, one Universalist, and twenty-six for a church of Christ.

"Your decision is wise," said the venerable chairman, "and I am happy to say that you will have the hearty sympathy of all the churches in New Albion. In many places, churches of this character are made to feel that they have no relation to any religious body, and their isolation becomes irksome to them; but it is not so with us; you will have as much fellowship with the Congregationalists as if you were a Congregational church, and as many friends among the Baptists as if you were a Baptist church, and so with all the rest. As our youngest sister, we shall all have a care for you, and shall be ready to lend you a hand, and we trust that the time will come when we shall be proud of you."

"I want to be a Methodist," said Mr. Thorpe, warmly, "just long enough to shout Amen to all that the Doctor has just said. I love my own church, but I love Christ's kingdom more; and God do so to me, and more also, if I ever lift my hand to divide the people of the Lord when they ought to dwell together in unity."

At the suggestion of Dr. Sampson, a committee of three, from those intending membership, was appointed to draw up a code of rules and a form of government for the new church. One of the members of the committee requested that Dr. Phelps might be added, but the Doctor asked that Mr. Strong, who had given much thought to problems of this nature, should be put in his place, and this was done.

The organization thus effected was somewhat unique. It was to be known as "The First Church of Christ in Cyprusville," that being the name fastened upon this innocent suburb by the treasurer of the corporation. Its only symbol of doctrine was the Apostles' Creed; its form of admission was extremely simple; its rules of procedure were not so elaborate as to invite to litigation. Besides the clerk and the treasurer of the church, there was a board of four wardens and four deaconesses, to supervise the religious and charitable work of the church. The secular affairs were in the care of a board of trustees. A meeting of all these officers, under the title of the "Official Board," over which the pastor was to preside, was to be held once a month for consultation. All important business must, however, be referred to the church. The weekly meeting, previous to each communion, was to be called the "covenant-meeting." Baptism was to be administered to adults by immersion or affusion, as the candidate might choose; as to infant baptism, no rule was made against it, but Mr. Strong advised that parents who wished their children baptized should have the rite performed at their homes, thus respecting the strongest scruple of the Baptist brethren. In case the church should call a pastor who was unwilling to administer this ordinance, the pastors of other churches in the city would cheerfully serve them.

It was not long before the new church was provided with a pastor. A Methodist clergyman, the Reverend Richard W. Gardner, a man of excellent character, who had been "located" without charge in New Albion on account of temporary disability, and who was known to be somewhat weary of itinerating, was easily persuaded to enter upon this work. No formal installation was deemed necessary, but services of recognition were held, in which the new church with its pastor was heartily received into the fellowship of all the churches. The next thing in order was the introduction of the pastor and three delegates into the Christian League. Most "Union" churches are either left out in the cold, or else enjoy a disclaimed and surreptitious fellowship with one of the sects, which exposes them to the suspicion of all the other sects; but this one stepped at once into a warm place already waiting for it, and seemed as truly to have "brought love" with it as a new baby does when it comes into a Christian family.

VI.

SOON after the organization of the church at Cyprusville, an episode occurred which tended not a little to strengthen the bonds of Christian fraternity in New Albion. The Methodist church had long been staggering under a load of debt. Its edifice, built in the flush times following the war, was an ambitious piece of architecture,— the church of the future, beyond a doubt, since it was much larger than the needs of its congregation,— and the pews were still vacant which the sanguine builders had expected to see occupied by the men who were to pay off the mortgages. Mr. Thorpe had carried this debt now for two years; it had been the burden of his days and the nightmare of his dreams. At length he had brought his congregation to the point of attacking it. He had made several anxious pilgrimages to rich Methodists in neighboring cities, but found small encouragement; it was evident that the Methodists in New Albion must shoulder their own load.

Accordingly, the first Sunday in October was devoted to a carefully planned effort for the payment of the debt. Mr. Thorpe had concluded to dispense with the services of a "finangelist," and to direct his own forces. There was to be no regular service in the church, but the people were invited to meet at ten o'clock in the forenoon, and, by the grace of God, the meeting would not adjourn, Mr. Thorpe said, until the debt was paid. A collation was provided in the basement, so that the people might spend the day in the work.

The debt amounted to thirty-two thousand dollars, and when the meeting opened in the morning seventeen thousand dollars were at once subscribed—this amount having been secured beforehand by private conference with the abler contributors. This excellent start awakened great enthusiasm, and, for a time, subscriptions came in rapidly; but long before noon the limit of the people's ability seemed to have been reached, and the list only footed up about twenty-four thousand dollars. Mr. Thorpe kept his forces well in hand, however, and showed no signs of wavering. Exhortations and appeals were interposed with singing; a judicious and energetic committee did a great deal of personal work with individuals; messengers were dispatched to labor with absentees. But it seemed evident that the large gifts had all been gathered in, and there was still a deficiency of more than seven thousand dollars that the small subscriptions yet to be obtained would by no means supply.

As Mr. Franklin walked home, after the morning service, with his pastor, they passed the door of the Methodist church.

"Let us look in a moment," said the parson, "and see how they are getting on."

They sat down in one of the back seats and watched the proceedings. From Mr. Thorpe's occasional remarks they learned the situation of affairs, and saw that the case was probably hopeless, though the resolute leader did not for a moment assent to such a conclusion.

As they walked away, Mr. Franklin said:

"Making a strong fight, aren't they?"

"Yes."

"But they will not take the fort."

"I don't know."

"I do; they've got to the sticking-point, and they will not get past it."

"Pity!" said Mr. Strong, sententiously.

After a moment's thought, Mr. Franklin added, with a new interest:

"Is it lawful to pull your fellow-creature out of a pit on the Sabbath day?"

"I should say so, especially when he is trying to get out himself."

"Lawful to hitch up your horse to pull him out?"

"Yes," laughed the minister.

"Well, you go home and get your lunch, and I'll get mine, and have Major put into the buggy. I'll be around there before one o'clock, and we'll see what we can do."

"All right."

It was not long before the good white horse came at a week-day pace to the door of the parsonage, and the friends were soon whirling away.

"Now, we've got to be swift," said the banker. "My first thought was to call only on some of our own people, but I am now inclined to give some of the rest a chance. The Episcopalians and the Free Baptists have a heavy debt of their own; the Adventists are not able to help much; we must enlist the others. Brinsmade must call on the First Church folks, Ellsworth on the Baptists, Thompson on the Universalists, you and I will look out for our own."

They were stopping at Mr. Brinsmade's door, and the master of the house answered the bell.

"We have set out," said Mr. Franklin, "to give the Methodists a little lift in paying their church-debt. Will you go and stand in the vestibule of your church and waylay as many as you can of your strongest men as they go into the afternoon service, and get subscriptions from them? Start the paper yourself. Then ask Dr. Phelps to take a collection before the sermon, for the same object. Get cash subscriptions, payable to-morrow at my bank. Report the amount to me at Mr. Strong's house by four o'clock sharp. Will you do it?"

"What a steam-boat you are!" said Brinsmade, laughing.

"Will you do it?" said Franklin, strenuously. "No time for nonsense, old fellow!"

"Yes, I'll do it."

"All right. Good-bye!"

And the white horse was soon flying down the street.

None of the other churches had afternoon services, and all that could be done in them must be done by personal application to a few of the more prosperous members. But Mr. Franklin had selected the right man as canvasser in each society, and after they had been set at work, he and his pastor returned to their own parish, which they divided between them, contriving, before four o'clock, to see a good proportion of its most generous members. At that hour, they all met at the parsonage, as by agreement, bringing with them a much larger sum than the most sanguine of them had hoped to get.

"They came down handsomely," said Brinsmade. "Three or four refused to give anything; but most of them had their names down before they knew it. It dropped on them so sudden like that they hadn't time to hunt up excuses. The old doctor warmed up to the business beautifully, and begged like a professional. I didn't suppose it was in him. They brought in nearly four hundred dollars in the boxes, besides all I got from individuals."

The others had much the same story to tell. Sympathy with the Methodists in their courageous effort was universal, and it had found a generous expression.

"Now each one of you sit down and write a short letter," said Mr. Franklin, "explaining that the amount you have collected is from friends in your church, naming the amount and stating where it may be called for to-morrow, and we'll go over at once and send the letters up to Brother Thorpe. I trust he is holding out yet, but it must be pretty tough for a man who doesn't believe in the perseverance of the saints to hang on to such a poor promise."

It was about half-past four when Mr. Franklin and his friends entered the Methodist church. The back seats were all occupied, so they stood in the space behind the pews and looked on. The church was pretty well filled, and Mr.

Thorpe was still keeping up a lively fire of appeal and argument; but there were no responses, and it was plain that hope had departed from most of the solicitors.

"Will you walk forward and take seats, gentlemen?" said one of them.

"No, thank you," answered Mr. Franklin. "We are only lobby members. How do you get on?"

"Slowly."

And the solicitor shook his head dolefully.

"How much have you got?"

"Only a little over twenty-five thousand."

"Why don't you stop where you are?"

"Then we lose everything. The greater share of the heavy subscriptions are conditional upon the raising of the whole debt."

"Wont your subscribers make them unconditional?"

"No. We've begged them to, but they are obstinate."

"Pity, isn't it?"

"Yes, sir. It will be a hard blow if we fail now."

The discouraged gentleman walked away. Mr. Franklin's air had been so indifferent that he had not ventured to ask him for anything.

"Send up your letter, Brinsmade," whispered Franklin. "Get that small boy to take it up."

The small boy toddled up the aisle and handed the envelope to Mr. Thorpe, who tore it open eagerly.

"Hallelujah!" shouted the impetuous Methodist. "Brethren, listen to this: 'The First Congregational Church of New Albion sends greeting to the First Methodist Church, with a pledge of sixteen hundred and seventy-five dollars, to be paid to-morrow at twelve o'clock noon by a check upon the First National Bank.' This is signed in behalf of the church by James W. Brinsmade."

The reading of the letter was followed by a storm of cheers and all the usual Methodist responses, in the midst of which the organ struck up the Doxology, and the whole congregation rose to their feet and sang it with a tremendous energy.

"Will Brother Brinsmade come forward?" shouted Mr. Thorpe. But before he had time to insist on this a little girl was mounting the pulpit with another envelope, which the pastor received with trembling hand. The noise hushed in a moment. This letter stated that five hundred and fifteen dollars, the gift of a few friends in the Universalist Church, would be on deposit the next day, at the same hour and the same place. Over this the furore was redoubled, one enthusiastic brother mounting a seat and calling for "the second verse of the Doxology!"

"Better not protract the agony," said Franklin to Ellsworth. "Let us send up our notes together."

The good minister, who had now for six hours been under a continuous nervous strain, in whose heart confidence had given way to anxiety and anxiety was beginning to change to discouragement, was so completely overcome by the contents of the other two envelopes that he sat down in his chair and could not speak for a moment, and at length rose and half sobbed out:

"Two more, brethren. One from friends in the Baptist Church, with a pledge of nine hundred and twenty-five dollars, and one from friends in the Second Congregational Church, with a promise of eighteen hundred and ten dollars. God bless them, every one!"

This time they were all too excited to sing, but there was a volley of amens in response to the last ejaculation, and men and women all over the house were laughing and crying like children.

"Give us the footing now, Brother Harrison," said the minister, at length, to the treasurer, who was keeping account of the subscriptions.

"Thirty thousand one hundred and fifty-five dollars," was the answer.

"Less than two thousand dollars more are wanted," cried Mr. Thorpe. "What do you say to that?"

"Two hundred dollars more for me!" was the first response from one of the heaviest subscribers; and then the supplementary subscriptions, large and small, came pouring in for ten minutes, faster than the treasurer could record them. As soon as there was a short pause, he summed up the amount again, and, rising to his feet, said quietly:

"Thirty-two thousand four hundred and sixty dollars—four hundred and sixty dollars for shrinkage!"

The scene that followed can only be imagined by those who know what an incubus a church-debt is to a devoted congregation, and who are also familiar with the ways in which Methodists are wont to express their feelings.

"I perceive," said Mr. Thorpe, rising to his feet after the tempest had subsided, "that all these pledges are to be paid to-morrow at noon at the First National Bank. It is easy to guess who is at the bottom of all this business, and I see him now standing near the door."

"No scenes for me," whispered the banker to his minister. "I'm going. Make my excuses." And he slipped out of the door and walked quickly away.

"Mr. Walter Franklin is the man," continued the parson, "and he is leaving the house at this moment; will not some one bring him back?"

But that was a vain suggestion. Mr. Franklin, as everybody knew, would not be brought back.

"Mr. Franklin's pastor must answer for him, then," said the minister; and Mr. Strong walked up the aisle amid great cheering. In a few graceful words, he told the congregation that Mr. Thorpe was right in his conjecture; that the plan of aiding them in their difficult undertaking was conceived and set in motion by Mr. Franklin, who had, nevertheless, been supported in the heartiest manner by the gentlemen on whom he had called; that the whole scheme was the inspiration of a moment and the fruit of a few hours' work; and that he trusted the result of it would be, not only the emancipation of the Methodist Church from the bondage of debt, but the strengthening of the bond of fellowship among the churches of New Albion. To that wish there were many fervent responses, and after a prayer of thanksgiving by the pastor, and the singing of "Blest be the tie that binds," the congregation broke up. That day will never be forgotten by any who had part in its doings, and the fruit of the seed then sown will be reaped in the increasing charity of many generations.

VII.

AT the November meeting of the League, the first suggestion came from Mr. Butterfield of the Free Baptist Church.

"I have been approached," he said, "by several of our active temperance workers, who greatly desire that the churches of this place shall unite in some movement for the promotion of their cause."

"What sort of movement?" asked Dr. Sampson.

"They did not say very definitely," was the answer. "They seem to think that the churches are not doing much for temperance, and that they ought to do more. I think they would like to have us open our churches Sunday evenings for a series of temperance meetings."

"And let them take the management of the meetings?" pursued the Doctor.

"I don't know, but I presume that they would be glad to be recognized in that way."

"No doubt; but I, for one, prefer to manage my own temperance meetings. The last time these people occupied my church they indulged in an amount of detraction and vituperation that I never wish to hear in my pulpit again."

Dr. Sampson's judgment was confirmed by several of the other pastors.

"Might we not, then," asked Mr. Butterfield, "unite our churches in working for temperance under a leadership furnished by themselves?"

"It seems to me," answered Mr. Franklin, "that this is impracticable. Union work in behalf of temperance is one of the hardest things in the world to secure. We can coöperate in ordinary religious work, because the lesson of toleration in religion has been learned, and because we are all ready to forget those things in which we differ; but, as respects the subject of temperance, there is, as yet, no such toleration; the sectarianism of temperance advocates is fully as violent as the sectarianism of the churchmen was a hundred years ago."

"Are you not rather rough on the temperance workers?" asked Mr. Thorpe.

"I do not mean to be. But just look at the facts. There are gentlemen in this club, I suppose, who sometimes use wine at their tables, and who, though they are careful to abstain from all excess, believe that they have a perfect right to use it as a beverage. There are other gentlemen in this club who regard every such use of it, no matter how careful, as a sin. I do not belong to either of these classes, but I can easily see that persons holding views so perfectly irreconcilable can never work together in promoting temperance. What is more, some of the gentlemen present are in favor of the passage of laws by which other persons in this company would be put into the category of criminals."

"Oh, come, Franklin, that's absurd! You don't mean that," cried Mr. Thorpe.

"I mean just that," persisted Franklin.

"But you know that the prohibitory law that some of us favor punishes the seller of liquor, not the drinker. There are no liquor-sellers in this room."

"A man cannot ordinarily drink wine without buying it, can he?"

"No, of course not."

"You wish to make it a crime to sell wine to be used as a beverage?"

"Yes."

"If it were a crime to sell, then the buyer would be morally *particeps criminis*, would he not?"

"I suppose so."

"Very well; there are gentlemen here who are in the habit of buying wine to be used as a beverage, and there are other gentlemen here who wish to make the selling of wine for that purpose a criminal act; how can these two classes of persons come to any understanding about temperance work? I am not discussing prohibition. I am not undertaking to justify or to condemn either of these classes of persons; I am only pointing out that the difference between them is, in its nature, insurmountable, and that they can only keep from quarreling about temperance work by ignoring the whole subject."

"Well, I guess you're right," said Mr. Thorpe, soberly.

"Not only is it impossible," the banker continued, "for these two classes to get on comfortably together, but any one who undertakes to mediate between them is liable to have his head broken. I dared to suggest, last summer, in a temperance meeting, that it was a gross blunder for the total abstainers to make war on all temperate drinkers,—to denounce them as malefactors and to hold them up to public reprobation; that it would be much easier to persuade than to coerce them into the ways of abstinence. For venturing that criticism, I was denounced as a toddy-drinker; and a crowded convention of reform clubs in our town hall applauded to the echo the assertion by one of their orators that I was worse than a rum-seller.

So you see that I have verified, in my own experience, the statement that toleration, in this field, does not exist. Not only is there no toleration for differences of theory or practice, there is no toleration for people who preach toleration and who try to bring about a better understanding. The time for coöperation in temperance work will come, but it is not yet."

" I am not ready to come to that conclusion," said Mr. Peters. "When an evil so great as the evil of intemperance exists in any community, it is humiliating to confess that the Christian people of the community are unable to combine against it."

" ' 'Tis true, 'tis pity; and pity 'tis 'tis true,' " said Mr. Franklin.

" But is there not one thing that can be done?" said Mr. Peters. " Can we not unite in enforcing the penal clauses of our present law against violators of them ? Our law forbids the sale of intoxicating liquors to minors and to intoxicated persons; it also forbids the selling of liquor on Sundays, and between twelve o'clock at night and five o'clock in the morning. To this extent it is a prohibitory law. Now, I am a prohibitionist; and I see no reason why I should not take the amount of prohibition this law allows me and make the most of it. We might enforce these clauses, if we would work together; we could make it dangerous to sell it to boys or to sell on Sundays. That would be a great gain; for it is notorious that there is more drinking done on Sunday than on any other day in the week, and that a great many of our boys are forming the drinking habit."

"That is good sense," said Dr. Strickland. "I am not a prohibitionist; I am not a total abstainer; I am one of the men who, as Mr. Franklin says, Mr. Peters seeks to put into the category of criminals,—though I don't mean to let that slight circumstance mar our friendly relations."

Here Peters arose, and extended his hand to the rector amidst much merriment.

"Notwithstanding the heresy of my opinions and the turpitude of my conduct in this matter of temperance," Dr. Strickland continued, "I am ready to do as much as any other man in this room in the line suggested by Mr. Peters."

"But what can we do?" asked Mr. Henderson.

"We can keep our eyes and ears open," answered Mr. Peters, "and report what we see and hear to the prosecuting agents. These gentlemen are appointed to enforce the law, but they do it very inefficiently,—for what reasons it is not necessary to inquire. It will do them good to know that a number of good citizens are carefully observing their operations. Let me give a bit of my own experience: I was passing along Jackson street the other day, in the rear of Pat Reilly's saloon, and I saw a little boy not more than seven years old come out of the back door with a pitcher in his hand and walk down the street. As I passed by him I said, carelessly, 'Hallo, bub! got some molasses?' 'No; beer!' he said. I walked right over to the office of Mr. Billings, our prosecuting agent, and told him what I had seen. He was disposed at once to take a high and mighty air, as of one with whose business I was meddling. He wanted to know how I knew that the purchase of the beer was not made by the child's father or some other adult then in the saloon; and whether this child's testimony would convict; and if I thought that what I had told him amounted to legal evidence. My answer was very brief. 'Do you believe,' I demanded, 'that I have told you the truth concerning what I saw?' 'Certainly,' he said. 'Very well,' I answered. 'If you accept that as truth, you are morally certain that liquor is illegally sold by Pat Reilly. You know it, and I know that you know it; if you haven't the legal evidence it is your business to get it. Good-morning.' If Mr. Billings should have a call of this sort every day or two, showing him that the people are watching the violations of the law and the manner of its enforcement, it would have a salutary effect upon him."

"That seems feasible," said Dr. Sampson. "One of the greatest curses of this liquor business is the laxity in the enforcement of law, to which it has given rise. Through our liquor legislation, the respect of the people for all law has been greatly weakened. Anything that we can do to add efficiency to the law will be valuable service."

The suggestion of Mr. Peters proved a fruitful one. The attention of the members of the club was called directly to numerous and glaring violations of the law; they took pains to inquire and to report concerning them; and a public sentiment was thus created which resulted in the more vigorous enforcement of law and in a considerable diminution in the amount of drunkenness.

VIII.

AS the winter drew on, the needs of the poor began to exercise the minds of benevolent persons in New Albion; there was great activity in several of the sewing societies, and the subject came to the front at the December meeting of the Christian League.

"Our constitution names the care of the poor as one of the proper subjects for conference at these meetings," said Dr. Strickland. "Just now there is a great amount of this work to do, not only in our own parish, but also in the district assigned to our church I wonder whether we are doing this work as effectively as it ought to be done. Little children, with scanty clothing and pinched faces, come to our door every day begging for food. It would be a burning shame to us if any should be left to suffer."

"By the way," said Mr. Strong, "what do you do for these children that come begging for food?"

"Feed them, of course," answered the rector. "We never give money to unknown beggars, and we never refuse food to any one, known or unknown, who asks for it at our door."

"I should like to know," Mr. Strong suggested, "how many of the members of this club adopt Mr. Strickland's rule in this matter."

The answers showed that it was the rule of the majority. One or two owned that they had no consistent method of dealing with such cases; most of the members concurred with Mr. Henderson when he said:

"I never could bring myself to refuse food to any person, old or young, who asked for it at my door. I could not refuse without feeling that I had disobeyed the command of Christ, 'Give to him that asketh thee.' I should blame myself if, with food in my house, I suffered any one to feel the pains of hunger."

"So far as the Lord's command is concerned," said Dr. Sampson, "it is not restricted to gifts of food; it is an unqualified rule, is it not?"

Mr. Henderson owned that it was.

"Why, then, does it not require you to give money as well as food to every one who asks for it?"

"I confess," said Mr. Henderson, "that my exegesis is not very clear; but it always seemed to me that gifts of food are somewhat different from gifts of money, and that while it is evidently injudicious to give money to beggars, it is a sin in this land of plenty to let anybody go hungry."

"But Paul says," Mr. Strong ventured, "'that if any man will not work, neither shall he eat.' That maxim, too, is unqualified."

"How about those who are out of work and can find no employment?" queried Mr. Thorpe.

"The rule does not apply to them. If 'any man *will not* work,' its language is. Those who, for any reason, are unable to earn their livelihood must be fed. But in many cases 'can't' is the mask of 'wont'; the inability to find work is the fruit of a disinclination to work; and when it becomes evident that indolence is the root of the trouble, then starvation is the apostolic remedy, and I believe that it is the right remedy."

"I can't stand by and see a man starve, no matter what his fault may be," protested Mr. Thorpe.

"I can," said Mr. Strong. "I shouldn't like to witness the suffering, but I would rather do it than violate that law of God which makes starvation the just penalty of idleness. We have set aside that law by our lazy and indiscriminate charities, and the consequence is a rapid increase of the pauper class in all our cities and large towns. It is time that we began to see the righteousness of that law, and to help in enforcing it, instead of helping men to evade it. There are just two things for us to do in this work of caring for the poor: We must make sure that no one who is both needy and helpless shall be allowed to suffer; and we must make it equally sure that no one who will not work shall escape suffering."

"But I do not see," said Dr. Strickland, "what this doctrine has to do with those little children who come to our doors for food. They are not able to earn their own livelihood; on Mr. Strong's principle, I ought to feed them."

"Have you taken pains," asked Mr. Strong, "to investigate the life of any of these children?"

"Why, yes; I have questioned them. One of the cases, for example, is that of a little girl whose father was killed in the war and whose mother is sick with rheumatism. She came to the door the other day when we were at dinner, and it was the first time I had seen her. The poor child was scantily clad, and had the most pitiful face I ever saw."

"What was her name?" asked Mr. Strong.

"I do not recall it."

"Was it Katy Macauley?"

"Yes; I think that was it."

"Did she tell where she lived?"

"Somewhere on James street, I think."

"Yes, that is likely. She gives a great many addresses, but never the true one. Her home is at the top of the brick block, on the corner of Swift and Thorne streets; her mother is a miserable drunkard, not an invalid at all, and she is wholly supported by what this child brings in. The clothing that Katy begs she peddles for money, and thus supplies herself with rum. Whether the father was killed in the war or not is known to nobody in this town; they have only lived here a few months; but it is certain that good Christian people who put food into Katy Macauley's basket are innocently helping to support the mother in vice and to doom the child to the life of a beggar. That is her calling now; what it will be by and by can be easily conjectured."

"You astound me," cried the good rector. "I had never dreamed of such a condition of things."

"This is not an exceptional case," continued Mr. Strong. "For more than two years my wife has followed home every child who has begged at our door, and she has yet to find a single instance in which the parents are not either drunkards or criminals, or both; and I have conferred with several intelligent persons in Bradford, and in other cities, who have made a study of such cases, and they tell me that children who beg, come, almost universally, from homes of vice and shame. People who are really deserving of charity do not send their children out to beg. The support of these wretched people in idleness is a great evil, but it is nothing compared with the wrong that is done in making it possible for them to bind their children to the trade of beggary."

"But you do come, now and then," said Mr. Peters, "on a pitiful case. A poor French woman came to me in great distress a few weeks ago. She stood weeping on the porch, and would not go in. It was difficult to learn her trouble, partly because her knowledge of English was imperfect, but chiefly on account of her grief and shame. Her husband had deserted her, leaving five young children to be provided for. She was in actual want. I followed her to her wretched home, and found things as she had represented them."

"What was her name?" asked Dr. Sampson.

"Duquette," answered Mr. Peters.

"Yes," said the Doctor; "I know them. But why did they appeal to you? They are in our visiting district, and their children attend our Sunday-school."

"One of them," answered Mr. Peters, "is a member of our Sunday-school."

"Where do they live?" asked Mr. Henderson.

"On Sands street." The answer was volunteered by three or four.

"The woman came to me, not long ago," said Mr. Henderson, "and our church has aided her once or twice."

"How many children did Mr. Peters find, on his visit to Mrs. Duquette?" Mr. Strong wished to know.

"I saw only three; the other two were not in."

"No," said Mr. Strong, "the other two are a boy of fifteen and a girl of sixteen, who were at work in one of the shoe-shops. They earn about twelve dollars a week. Add to this the amount given to this family by three churches within the last few weeks, and the liberal weekly orders given them by the town overseers of the poor, to whom they have applied for aid, and you will see that Mrs. Duquette has been substantially comforted for the loss of her husband, who has indeed run away."

The laughter that followed this exposure was at the expense of so many people that it could afford to be hearty and general.

"Nevertheless, brethren," said Dr. Sampson, "we have the poor always with us — Christ's poor as well as the other kind ; and the duty of finding them out and administering to them is not to be neglected."

"Not only so," added Mr. Strong; "these very people that we have been talking about appeal to our charity quite as strongly as those whom we call the worthy poor. We must take care that they do not subsist in idleness and vice upon our gifts. Of material aid they need but little, though sometimes, even to them, a little help of this sort in starting on a new career may not be amiss; but they need friendship more than anything else in the world,— a firm, sensible, honest, patient friend, who will show them a better way of living, and lead them into it, is, for every one of these wretched families, the one thing needful. The discovery that a large class of people exists among us who are harmed by the indiscriminate bestowment of money or material aid is no sign that less charity is called for; not less, but more is demanded, only it must take a different form. I find no difficulty whatever in accepting Christ's unqualified rule of charity: 'Give to him that asketh thee.' Give to every beggar, I say; give him what he needs most, and satisfy yourself, before you give him anything, what are his deepest needs. If money will do him the most good, give him money; if food or clothing will do him the most good, give him food and clothing; but if you study his case, you will probably find that the aid most needed is moral rather than physical. Some direction the man may require, and some encouragement, and much bracing of his will, and not a little rousing of his self-respect. If there is any kind of Christian work more imperative than this, I do not know where to find it. And there is enough of it to do. The problem of pauperism confronts us. In all our larger towns we find a growing class of those who are willing to subsist without work. The slipshod way in which official relief is generally given by the civil authorities encourages pauperism. The effect of our large system of industry, which builds up great corporations and gathers into tenement houses a vast homeless population that drifts about from place to place and never takes root anywhere, is, I greatly fear, to develop pauperism. So we have among us a large number of these discouraged, unthrifty, hapless people, some of whom have begun to ask for alms, and some of whom have asked so often that mendicancy has become chronic with them. It takes but a short time for a family to sink down from self-respect to beggary, and, once in that slough, it is very hard to get out. Last winter, our overseers of the poor granted outdoor relief to more than one thousand different persons—one in fifteen of the whole population.

The times were hard, but these figures must include not a few whose poverty arose from a defect of will. This shows us what a work we have to do, and I heartily agree with Dr. Strickland in thinking that it is high time we were about it. Excuse me, gentlemen, for inflicting on you a lecture, but the subject is one in which I am deeply interested."

"How are we to deal with this problem?" said Mr. Franklin.

"We need but little additional machinery," said Dr. Sampson. "The town is already divided geographically among the churches; each church ought to subdivide its territory, and assign to each small district one or two visitors. There ought to be a central committee, meeting weekly during the winter, and consisting of one person from each church. This committee should have an office, at which a record should be kept of all the cases aided, with full particulars of each case,—a record open to the inspection of visitors only. It would be better to have a common relief fund, under the control of the committee; visitors to grant only temporary relief, until they had laid the case fully before the committee. It would be necessary to have a secretary, who should keep the register, and who should be in the office at certain hours every day. Then the people should be pledged, if possible, to give no money, food, or clothing to unknown persons, but to refer every applicant to this secretary, who should put the case at once into the hands of the visitor in whose district the applicant lived. The secretary would need a map of the town, with the boundaries of each sub-district, and the name and address of its visitor. Thus all applications for alms could at once be investigated, and that over-lapping of charity, on which pauperism thrives, would not be possible."

"The Doctor's scheme seems rational and feasible," said Mr. Franklin. "Can we not have the members of such a central committee chosen by the churches this very week?"

To this question there was no negative.

"Then," said the banker, "I trust the Doctor himself will attend the first meeting of the committee, and submit his sketch of an organization; and that the churches will speedily subdivide their territory and appoint their visitors. No time should be lost."

"You've got some work to do," said Dr. Strickland, "in enlightening the community. Most of us have loose notions of what charity is. This talk has helped me, but the majority of my neighbors are as much in the dark as I was an hour ago."

"This is true," Mr. Strong added, "not only

of the church people, but also of all those persons who sneer at the churches and who boast a religion of 'good works.' The man who does not go to church, but who gives the poor family his ton of coal or his barrel of flour, off hand, and no questions asked, is the hero of a certain class. It will be difficult to make them see that their hero is doing about five times as much harm as good, and that what these poor people need is not tons of coal or barrels of flour, but time and thought and patient friendship. But if any man, saint or sinner, wants to follow Jesus Christ, this is the path by which he can come nearest to him.

IX.

IN pushing its campaign for the suppression of drunkenness and pauperism in New Albion, the club soon found the need of a work more radical than any it had yet attempted. The streets of the town were thronged every evening with young men from the mills, whose homes were cheap boarding-houses, and to whom the saloons offered about the only place of resort. To prevent or punish the sale of strong drink to such of them as were under age was well, so far as it went; but the call for more efficient measures for restraining and saving those young men and boys began to make itself heard.

"What we want," said Mr. Biddle, one of the delegates from the First Church, "is a Young Men's Christian Association."

"Have you never had one in New Albion?" inquired Mr. Thorpe.

"Oh, yes," answered Mr. Biddle, "we had a flourishing association here for several years—rooms in Stone's Block; had a secretary who gave his whole time to the work; held several conventions here; sent delegates to all the international conventions; went myself once as a delegate."

"What became of it?"

"Oh, it died about five years ago."

"What ailed it?"

"Well, I don't know. People seemed to lose interest in it; workers dropped off; took the secretary pretty much all the time to raise money to pay his own salary and the rent; the thing fell through."

"But if it was occupying its field and doing its work, I should have thought that the people of New Albion would have refused to let it die."

"That was exactly the trouble," answered Dr. Sampson. "If the association had confined itself to work for the benefit of the young men of the town,—providing them a safe place of resort, and pleasant companionship, and wholesome diversion, and good religious influences,—it would have justified and prolonged its life. But, led by certain zealous brethren, it undertook to do a great many other things. It began to hold gospel meetings at the jail and the poor-house, and outdoor meetings in the park and in the groves on Sunday; it undertook to establish mission schools here and there; it began a series of evangelistic meetings in every town in the county; it seemed ambitious to take into its hands the entire management of religious affairs in all this region. Instead of being a society whose object was to work for young men, it became a society whose chief object was to afford a few zealous young men, and a large number who were no longer young, an opportunity to exercise their gifts of speech in various places for the general benefit of the human race. It spread itself so thin that it finally soaked in and disappeared."

"But could we not have a new organization, and avoid the old mistakes?" asked Mr. Biddle.

"Possibly," replied the Doctor. "Yet it seems to me that the distinctively religious work in behalf of our young men can be done as well by the churches, and that the thing we most want is some sort of a place in which young men may safely spend their evenings together."

"That is what you want," said Mr. Franklin; "and about half the young fellows you want to get in will be kept away from such a place if it purports to be a religious resort. In vain is the net of a Christian Association spread in the sight of most of these birds. But if you would open, say, a 'Young Men's Union Club,' they would come into that; that wouldn't be a scarecrow."

It is not necessary to detail the conversations that followed. There was considerable difference of opinion about methods; but after two or three conferences a plan was matured by which a building, devoted to the young men of New Albion, was erected on the main street of the town. It was built by private subscription, and was held and managed by a self-perpetuating board of trustees. On the front of the building, cut into the stone, was the simple legend, "Young Men's Club." The first floor was occupied by a coffee-room, a smoking-room, a chess-room, and a reading-room. The second story front room was a library and correspondence room, and the large room in the rear was a gymnasium, which, with a supply of camp-chairs, could be speedily converted into a lecture-hall.

The club was not free, save that the coffee-room, opening on the street, was for the use of the public. Refreshments were furnished at low prices — a good cup of coffee with a sandwich for five cents. For the privileges of the other rooms, and for all the advantages of the club, members paid fifty cents a quarter. For the gymnasium there was a small extra charge. It was found that the young men prized the club the more because it was not free, not wishing to be mendicants in their pleasures. A large number of the young men of the churches joined the club, and took part in its various literary enterprises and diversions. Before the end of its first year it had a membership of several hundred, and had begun to prove a formidable rival to the liquor shop and the minstrel show.

To another of the enterprises set on foot by the Christian League only a passing word can be given. That was the establishment, in one of the poor districts, of a free kindergarten. Dr. Strickland had visited some of these schools in Boston, and had come back full of enthusiasm for this method of charity. "It is a great discovery," he said. "No other work promises such results in the salvation of the poor. If you can get the little children out of the squalid homes into a clean and bright place, and keep them there four or five hours a day, under the care of patient, cheerful, loving women, who never beat nor scold them,—who teach them the first principles of courtesy and kindness and self-control, and keep them happy with pictures and games and marches and songs,—if you can keep them under such influences until they are six or seven years old, impressions are likely to be made upon their characters that will never be erased. The memory of these happy years will be a daily blessing to them. Besides, through the children, you get such access to their parents as you could secure in no other way; and the children themselves carry the gospel of neatness and gentleness into their homes—the best missionaries you can find. One kindergarten is worth more in the way of civilizing and Christianizing these Arabs in embryo than six mission Sunday-schools. One hour a week doesn't amount to much; four hours a day really tells on a child's life."

Dr. Strickland was so thoroughly in earnest, and he brought so much testimony to support his project, that funds enough were easily raised to set the kindergarten a-going. Once at work, it so completely proved its beneficence and justified Dr. Strickland's faith in it, that the churches all rejoiced to bear a share in its support; as its numbers grew, its quarters were enlarged and more teachers were employed; now, at the end of three years, every citizen is ready to testify to a great improvement in the manners and the morals of that depraved district in the midst of which the kindergarten stands.

X.

IT must not be supposed that the Christian League Club had lived and wrought all these years in New Albion and been heard of by nobody. Its members took no pains to advertise its doings, neither did they have any secrets. Many things had come to pass of late in this thriving town; a new spirit of coöperation and of enterprise had taken possession of the churches; their power was more perfectly concentrated and more effectively expended than ever before, and the results were beyond question or cavil. The source from which these good works proceeded could not be hid. At first, there was a disposition on the part of some of the uninvited to speak skeptically about "secret conclaves" and "close corporations," but as it became evident that nothing nefarious was hatched in these conferences, that the club assumed no power, and only served as an apparatus for generating and directing public opinion, and that its conclusions had no more force than there might be in the reasons by which they were supported, the ungraciousness of finding fault was recognized by most sensible persons, and the club became a highly popular organization. A little conversation which occurred one day between Captain Conover, a Baptist, and Dr. Duncan, a Methodist, in the office of the latter, fairly illustrates the public sentiment.

"The fact is," said the captain, " that we haven't got but one church here in New Albion. There are several different meetin'-houses, and several different congregations, and they have various ways of workin' and worshipin', but there aint but one church. We all stan' together pretty solid, I tell 'em. We all move as one body. There aint any pushin' of Baptist interests or Meth'dist interests, or Congregational interests or 'Piscopal interests; the only thing we're pushin' is the kingdom of heaven. I tell you what it is, it's ben a-comin' faster these three last years 'n I ever see it come before."

As the captain's heart warmed, his dialect strengthened.

"You are right," responded the Doctor. "We've got things on a very good basis. I was afraid that when Brother Thorpe went away we might get a minister who wouldn't work in so well with the rest; but Brother Hartwell seems to have been fairly captured by the League, and he will do his part, you may depend. As for the Methodist laymen of New Albion, you can always count on them. They have some solid reasons for thinking well of this club. It will take them a good while to forget that Sunday afternoon when the little chaps walked up the aisle of our church, one after another, with the letters that proclaimed to us deliverance from our bondage of debt. I don't think so much of shouting as some of our folks do, but I shouted then as loud as the loudest of them."

"Well," said the captain, "this new way is a pretty old way after all, I guess. It's about the way they did it in Ephesus and Antioch, when the disciples was called Christians,—not Baptists nor Meth'dists. There was only one church there, 'n' yit like enough there was half a dozen congregations. P'r'aps they didn't all have jest the same rules, nor jest the same ways of worshipin', but they all worked together. This is the kind of Christian union that plain and sensible folks believe in. Some of the brothering that run the machines don't think much on 't; but the rank 'n' file are sound. We've been a-prayin' for years that all Christ's disciples might be one, and makin' no end of talk about it, but it was mostly talk; now we've got down to business."

Captain Conover was a sort of village oracle, and his shrewd comments reflected the prevailing opinion.

Not only within the precincts of New Albion, but beyond its borders, the unity of its churches became a theme of conversation. In three or four of the larger towns in the neighborhood, similar clubs had been formed, and the experiences of New Albion were repeated with some variations. The notion that the relations of Christian churches ought to be those of coöperation rather than of competition, began to get a firm lodgment here and there in Bradford County. The small country towns, back among the hills, away from the railroads, were the places into which it was hardest for the new gospel to find entrance. In many of these towns, with populations of less than a thousand persons, there were from three to five churches,—sometimes two of the same sect. The members of these churches generally regarded the peculiarities of their several sects as matters of supreme importance, and repelled with heat any suggestion of closer relations between the churches. The narrowness of the laity in these towns was not likely to be mitigated by their religious teachers,—the feebleness of the churches making it difficult for them to secure pastors of intelligence and breadth,—though this rule was not without shining exceptions.

One Monday forenoon, in November, Mr. Strong with Mr. Hartwell, the new Methodist minister, a man of fine scholarship and excellent spirit, had dropped in at Dr. Sampson's study, and were holding a rather jovial conference with him, when a weather-beaten covered buggy stopped opposite the house, and a venerable man, with a clean-shaven face and a fringe of gray beard under his chin, passed by the window of the study and rang the bell.

"That's Father Crane, of Monroeville," said the Doctor, going to the door; "come in, Father Crane; come right into the study; I want you to know my friends;" and the Rev. Jonas Crane, pastor of the Baptist Church in Monroeville, was formally presented to the other two clergymen and cordially received by them.

"You must have got an early start," said Mr. Strong, "to have driven eighteen miles this morning."

"Somewhat early," said Father Crane, slowly and precisely. "The denizens of the rural communities find it necessary to use the prime of the morning, and I awake no earlier than is the wont of my parishioners."

"Morning comes a little earlier to the folks on the top of Monroeville hill than it comes to us dwellers in the valley," said Dr. Sampson.

"New ideas strike you up there a little earlier than they do us, I suppose," said Dr..Hartwell, smiling.

Father Crane's face darkened.

"I trust not," he said. "We are not much given to novelties. The old gospel is commensurate to all our exigencies."

At this moment the servant appeared at the study door, announcing that a caller was inquiring for Mr. Strong. The latter, begging to be excused, went out into the hall and soon returned, bringing the caller with him.

"Oh, no; ceremonies are off," he was saying. "Come right in! Dr. Sampson, this is the Reverend Mr. Slade, of the Congregational Church in Monroeville; Mr. Hartwell, of the Methodist Church; you know your neighbor, doubtless." The greeting of Father Crane and Mr. Slade was not unfriendly, but somewhat constrained.

This irruption had not subsided when Mr. Hartwell was called out in the same way, and returned, rejoicing, bringing his man with him.

"You can't outvote me any longer," he said; "the Methodist reënforcements have arrived," and he introduced the Reverend Mr. Towne, of the Methodist Church in Monroeville; whereupon there was hilarity, into which the three ministers from New Albion seemed to enter with rather more spirit than the three ministers from Monroeville.

"Well!" said Mr. Strong, putting that syllable into a heavy expiratory blast, "Monroeville has come down upon us this morning like the wolf on the fold."

"And for the very same reason that the wolf came down, I suspect," said Mr. Slade.

"Hunger, eh?" suggested Mr. Strong. "Getting starved out, are you?"

"My brethren can speak for themselves," said Mr. Slade; "but that's about my case."

"So I inferred from your last letter. And I have a shrewd suspicion that all you Monroeville pastors are here upon the same errand."

"Father Crane had written to me," said Dr. Sampson, "that he wished to consult me with reference to a grant from our Home Evangelization fund."

"Under these circumstances," said Mr. Towne, "I need not blush to confess that I have come down hoping to obtain a few subscriptions from Mr. Hartwell's people toward making up the deficiency in our accounts."

"This is a remarkable coincidence," said Dr. Sampson. "I am inclined to call it providential. And now we are here, all together, it is a good time to have a frank talk about the work in Monroeville."

"How large a town is Monroeville?" asked Mr. Hartwell.

"About a thousand inhabitants," answered his Methodist brother.

"Eight hundred and twenty-three in 1870," said Dr. Sampson, referring to a gazetteer. "The population is not increasing, I presume?"

"No; it is falling off," answered Mr. Slade.

"Any other churches besides your three?"

"No; the Episcopalians have a small interest and the Adventists also; but neither society has a meeting-house, and neither has a pastor. They hold occasional services in a hall."

"Five religious societies, a population of eight hundred and twenty-three: exactly one hundred and sixty-four souls and three-fourths of a soul for each society."

This was Mr. Strong's arithmetic.

"But when we remember," said Dr. Sampson, "that not more than three-fifths of the population of any town *can* attend church on any Sunday, we reduce the number of possible churchgoers to less than one hundred for each congregation."

"I suppose," said Mr. Hartwell, "that there are many families in your town that are not connected with any of your churches."

"Of course," answered Mr. Slade.

"How large a proportion of your people, do you think, are outside all these societies?"

"Counting in the Roman Catholics, of whom there is now a sprinkling, I should say one-third."

Further questioning brought out the fact that

the aggregate membership of the three Monroeville churches represented on this occasion was ninety-eight, and the total number of persons present on a fair Sunday morning about one hundred and thirty. It was also testified that the salary of the Congregational pastor was five hundred dollars, two hundred and fifty of which was contributed by the home missionary organization of the county; that the Baptist parson's salary was four hundred dollars, of which one hundred and fifty came from a similar source; and that the Methodist minister subsisted on three hundred and fifty dollars, a portion of which he collected every year by visiting well-to-do Methodists in neighboring towns.

"Now, let us figure a little," Mr. Strong proposed. "The population of Monroeville is not more than eight hundred and twenty-three; the population of New Albion is not less than thirteen thousand; Monroeville has five religious societies, and makes no provision for its Roman Catholics; New Albion has ten, including the Roman Catholic Church. If we had as many churches in proportion to our population as you have, how many churches would there be in New Albion? As eight hundred and twenty-three is to thirteen thousand, so is five to the answer. Cipher it out, Brother Towne. What do you make it?"

"Seventy-eight."

"Yes; that is the number of churches we should have in New Albion, if we were as liberal in our allowance to ourselves of religious privileges as the people of Monroeville are to themselves."

"You don't mean that," protested Mr. Slade.

"Oh, you needn't lay it to me," answered the other. "I haven't invented these facts. I'm not responsible for them. The question is not what I mean, but what the good people of Monroeville mean."

"Your comparisons are odious," laughed Mr. Slade. "But they are not quite fair. We have really but three churches in Monroeville."

"Count out your Episcopalians and your Adventists, then," persisted Mr. Strong. "I doubt whether it is fair to do it, for it is a question whether their congregations are not nearly as large as some of yours; but leave them out of the account and recast the proportion, and it will give us forty-seven churches as our lawful share in New Albion, provided your standard is a good one. Are your people any richer than ours?"

"I doubt it."

"Is the valuation of your town, *per capita*, greater than ours?"

"I couldn't say, but I should guess not."

"No use in guessing," said Dr. Sampson; "here are the figures in our State reports, and it is a simple sum in division. The valuation of Monroeville, *per capita*, is exactly four hundred and one dollars, and of New Albion six hundred and seven."

"We are much better able, then," Mr. Strong went on, "to have fifty churches than you are to have three, and what would be said of us if we undertook to maintain fifty separate church organizations in this town? Our ten churches amply provide for all the wants of this community."

"You are bearing down heavily upon us, Brother Strong," said Mr. Towne. "But there are some features of the situation that you do not take into the account. You must remember that these churches on the hills have long been the nurseries in which many of the members of your city churches have been trained. Our young men grow up under the influences of these small churches, and as soon as they are grown they depart to the cities and the large towns. The training they receive while they are with us fits them to be useful men wherever they may go. You will find that the bone and sinew of your own church was reared on these hills."

"I am quite familiar with that fact," replied Mr. Strong, "and I do not wish to leave it out of the account. That churches ought to be supported in the small country towns needs no argument; the only question is whether you need five times as many churches, in proportion to the population, as we find necessary in the larger towns."

"But our population is scattered over a large territory."

"How far apart are those two of your churches that are farthest apart?"

"About a mile."

"Do the people pay much attention to the question of distance in selecting their churches?"

"I cannot say that they do."

"Do those, for example, who live nearer the Methodist Church than any other, all or nearly all, attend the Methodist Church?"

"Oh, no."

"Practically, then, so far as distance is concerned, the people of the town, take them all together, would be as well served by one church, located at some central point, as they are now?"

"Nearly so; yes."

While this conversation had been going on, Father Crane had been nervously stroking his bald head. Like the dove, he had found no rest for the sole of his foot, though he had sought it for both of them by many nervous shifts of his left leg over his right, and *vice versâ*. At length, he ventured to say:

"Brother Strong seems strangely oblivious of the circumstance that Christian people, in the rural communities as well as the urban, have convictions of their own respecting the doctrines and ordinances of religion which they consider themselves under obligation to maintain. We have, in Monroeville, those who are Baptists because of unfeigned and unalterable persuasion; and Congregationalists, I presume, of whom a similar state of mind might be predicated; and Methodists, who also devotedly desiderate their own peculiar forms and ceremonies. Why have we not an equal right with the dwellers in more populous places to indulge our predilections?" Father Crane's rather pompous sentences were full of the warmth of sincerity.

"Our venerable brother goes for the root of the matter the first time," said Mr. Strong, instinctively opposing his homespun idioms to the country parson's Johnsonese. "The reason why there are three churches in Monroeville instead of one, is that everybody thinks he must have his pet notions gratified in the fashion of church life and work. These fashions, like many other fashions, may well enough be followed if folks can afford it. Here's my neighbor, with wages enough to live in comfort if they are wisely expended. But he thinks that his wife must have just so many ribbons on her bonnet and so many laces on her cloak, and that his girls must have just such a style of shoes; and so much money goes for all these fine fixings that he has to come around once or twice a year and ask his neighbors for flour and coal."

"But," protested the old gentleman, "you do not intend to insinuate that there is any similitude between the vain adornments you have mentioned and the distinctive principles of a religious denomination!"

"That is exactly what I mean. Ribbons and laces are not necessarily vain adornments. They are beautiful, and may be indulged in with thanksgiving if one does not sacrifice in getting them that which is of more consequence. In like manner, the various denominational peculiarities are innocent enough; but they add nothing to the real value of the gospel of Christ, any more than the laces add warmth to the cloak. Believing in these denominational peculiarities does no man any good whatever. It nourishes no man's manhood; it saves no man's soul. The only effect of exalting these things is to belittle the manhood and to shrivel the soul. Yet it is by exalting these small distinctions that the Christians of Monroeville maintain three churches where there is barely room for one."

"You fail to see some of the aspects of this case," said Mr. Slade. "I have always thought it better for every family to have a home by itself, even though it may cost a little more than it would to put three or four families together in the same house. I would rather have my own fire and my own table and my own family altar. Such an arrangement is in the interest of peace and happiness."

"I thank you for that illustration," answered Mr. Strong, "because it is familiar, and because I wish to show that it wholly misses the point. The Christians in Monroeville do not belong to three families. They are all members of one family. The case is like this: An old mother and two daughters have income enough to live together in comfort. But there are some small matters about which they disagree. They like the same kind of bread, but one wants the loaves round, and another prefers them square, and a third insists on twists. They all wish to burn coal, but one desires a grate, and one a baseburner, and one a sheet-iron stove. Their differences are all of this nature. They love one another dearly — so they say; they often get together and tell one another how much they have in common, and yet they insist on living apart. The rent of three houses must be paid, three fires must be fed, three lamps must burn; the expense of living for the three is more than twice as much as it would be if they all lived together. Their income will not support them. So every year they go around among the neighbors and take up a collection to enable them to keep up these three separate establishments. Is it any wonder that the wisdom of this management does not always appear to the persons who are asked to subscribe?"

"You disapprove of denominations, then?" queried Elder Crane.

"Let us stick to Monroeville for the present," Mr. Strong proposed. "The real question now is whether there ought to be three churches in Monroeville."

"Of course," said Mr. Slade, "if you come to that, there ought not to be more than one,— but——"

"Well, go on; complete your statement."

"The real difficulty is to know which two of these churches ought to commit suicide for the benefit of the third. Wendell Phillips tells a story of the discontented wife who said, 'They tell us that in the eyes of the law the man and his wife are one, but I've found out that the man's the one.' I suppose that the Congregationalists of Monroeville are all agreed that there ought to be but one church in that town, and that the Congregational church is the one;

and that the Baptists have the same opinion about their church, and the Methodists ditto. For my part, I own that I am inclined to stand with my own people. Ours is the old church. Your parable of the mother and daughters fits in here. The girls ought to have staid in the homestead."

"I don't know about that. There was a real justification, fifty or a hundred years ago, for the formation of new societies here in New England. The protest of the Baptists against the State church, and of the Methodists against the hyper-Calvinism and the frigidity of the Standing Order were right and reasonable. They did a good service in coming out from the Old Church and lifting up their standards. In view of that service they are entitled, I think, to just as much consideration as the Congregationalists in the settlement of this problem of consolidation. But the real reasons for separation no longer exist. The things against which they protested have disappeared. Your Calvinism, Slade, would never trouble the stoutest Arminian; and the same thing is true of nine-tenths of the Congregational ministers. The old frigidity is gone from our worship; we sing and talk and pray in our social meetings as freely, if not quite so fervidly, as our Methodist brethren; women are finding their voices; the old lines that separated the two sects are substantially obliterated; the old difference between us and the Baptists with reference to State support no longer exists; and our ministers now generally immerse all who desire it. There is a deeper difficulty with respect to communion not yet overcome, but I have strong hopes that even this will not be suffered to stand in the way of consolidation in the small towns."

"So far as I am concerned," said Dr. Sampson, "I am not prepared to abandon the Baptist ground on this subject; but in view of the mischiefs arising from division in small communities, I am ready to go to the verge of my principles in promoting unity."

"Is it not true, brethren," Mr. Strong went on, "that the real differences of doctrine and of worship among the Christians of Monroeville are wholly insufficient to warrant the existence of three separate churches?"

Mr. Towne and Mr. Slade at once confessed, and denied not. Elder Crane was less acquiescent.

"I am now an old man," he said, "and I do not readily accommodate myself to new measures. I acknowledge the justice of much that Mr. Strong has urged,—especially the historical references that he has adduced; but I could not consent to have my little church on the hill abandoned. There are too many precious memories." The old clergyman paused, and there were tears in his voice as well as in his eyes. In a moment he went on: "My time is nearly come, however. One part of my errand to-day was to consult about laying down the burden that has become too heavy for me. And I shall not stand in the way of any plans of re-organization which my people may wish to adopt."

"I understand and respect the feeling of Elder Crane," said Mr. Strong. "The old associations are sacred. It is hard to give up the old home. But when it costs for repairs more than we can possibly raise, and we are in danger of being buried in its ruins, judgment must prevail over sentiment."

"But here's the rub," said Mr. Towne. "How are you going to make the people of Monroeville see this thing as you do?"

"With your help," answered Mr. Strong, "the thing can be done. Will you not confer together, and then call on us for any help we can render? We have learned, you know, here in New Albion, how to dwell together in unity, and we would be glad to show our neighbors how they may go and do likewise."

The two younger ministers of Monroeville promised to look it over, and to see what could be done, and thus the conference ended.

XI.

THE report of the conversation in Dr. Sampson's study furnished a theme for the next meeting of the club.

"Since our talk that morning," said Dr. Sampson, "I have taken great pains to get at a few of the facts about the small towns in this county. Monroeville is the type of a class. There is Stapleton, with a population of eleven hundred and with four churches; Scantico, with six hundred people and three churches; Rowell, with nine hundred people and four churches; and so on. Eight towns in this county, with an aggregate population of nine thousand one hundred and thirty-four, support thirty-seven religious societies. Of these, at least fifteen are receiving more or less aid from the various home missionary organizations."

"Even when the societies are self-supporting," said Dr. Phelps, "the support is generally meager, the membership is small, and the terms of the pastorates are lamentably short."

"It is plain," said Mr. Hartwell, "that the churches in these small towns ought to unite. What hinders them?"

"First," answered the Doctor, "is the strength of the sectarian prejudice,—always more intense in the small places than in the large ones. Then there is a sentiment much less reprehensible,—the attachment to the local organization, around which many grateful memories cling. The people do not like to give up a church which may have a noble history, and which is sure to be the shrine of sweet associations."

"Certainly," said Mr. Hartwell; "those hinderances are obvious. They may be called sentimental; even so, they are not easily overcome. Are there any other practical obstacles?"

"In most of these towns," said Mr. Peters, "the only way of uniting would be to abandon the old organizations and form a new one,—a union church, like ours at Cyprusville."

"But do you know," Mr. Franklin broke in, "that it is legally impossible to do anything of the sort?"

"What do you mean?" demanded three or four voices.

"Just what I say. The union of two churches of different denominations is a proceeding so rare that no provision for it is made, so far as I can learn, in our statutes, nor in those of any other State. Secular corporations can be legally consolidated, but church corporations cannot be. Christian union seems to be regarded by our legislators as against public policy. Churches have sometimes been brought together, but the act was unwarranted by law. Any troublesome member of either church could have procured an order from the courts tearing them apart again."

"Then," said Mr. Strong, "it is high time that we had an act before the Legislature, enabling churches to obey the Christian law. I hope that unanimous consent will be given to the appointment, by this club, of Mr. Franklin as our agent, to secure the passage of such a law at this session."

Consent was readily given. Concerning the work of Mr. Franklin in the lobby of the Connecticut Legislature the historian of the club is not fully informed; but the facts to be recorded below indicate that he must have been successful.

"There is another practical difficulty," said Mr. Franklin, picking up the thread of the discussion where Mr. Peters had dropped it, "more serious than the legal disability. When you have got your union churches formed, they belong nowhere. Now, people like to feel that they do belong somewhere. If they are weak and small themselves, they enjoy the knowledge that they are members of some respectable body in whose interests they have a part. These union churches have nowhere to go, unless we invite them into our Congregational conferences, as we generally do. But then the other sectarians say that a union church is nothing but a Congregational church. There is truth enough in what they say to make it necessary to devise some means by which these union churches may find a less ambiguous fellowship; and I propose a convention of all the churches in the county, to meet twice a year, for consultation about Christian work in the county."

"Who should call such a convention?" asked Mr. Hartwell.

"This Club," answered Mr. Franklin. "A committee, consisting of the minister and one layman from each of our churches, should issue the call, summoning every church in the county to send its pastor and a lay delegate to such a convention, at which a permanent organization should be effected."

"What churches should we invite?"

"I would put the Apostles' Creed into the call, and send it to every church in the county,— Protestant or Roman Catholic,—with a sentence explaining that any church which accepts this creed and conforms to it in its teaching would be welcome in the convention."

"Do you suppose that the Romanists would come?" queried Dr. Strickland.

"I fear they would not; but I would invite them."

"Would you dare to open the doors to heretics?" asked Mr. Peters.

"Any church that makes its teachings conform to the Apostles' Creed is orthodox enough for me. I mean that I am willing to make that Creed the basis of union in Christian work. Are not you?"

"I'm not at this moment prepared to say that I would not."

"I trust," said the banker, dryly, "that you never will be any better prepared than you are at this moment."

The club discussed the proposed convention vigorously for an hour, and then, no one dissenting, the committee was appointed and the call was speedily issued. The object of the convention, as stated in the call, was "to promote union and efficiency in Christian work, and to secure a more systematic evangelization of the destitute neighborhoods throughout the county." The organization effected was simple. It was named "The Christian League of Bradford County." The only permanent officer was the secretary. An Outlook Committee of five was to be appointed at each meeting, whose duty it should be to make inquiry respecting the feeble churches, and to secure, so far as possible, coöperation or consolidation. Meetings were to be held twice a year, on the first Tuesdays of April and October. Papers and addresses showing the waste and mischief caused by sectarian divisions, and the need of unity, were to be provided by the Outlook Committee for each meeting. The principal object of the League, as defined in the preamble, was "to generate and disseminate right opinions respecting the duty of Christians to coöperate, to see that the waste places are cultivated, and to extend the fellowship of all believers to those churches that have no denominational fellowship."

There was some hesitation, at first, about this project; but the representatives of the New Albion churches all threw themselves into it with such heartiness that the doubts and scruples of the rest were vanquished, and the constitution was adopted with some enthusiasm.

Not many days after this, a letter from Monroeville invited a deputation from the churches of New Albion to come up and hold a public meeting in the interests of Christian union. The three ministers who had part in the accidental conference in Dr. Sampson's study responded to this call, taking with them Dr. Strickland, of the Episcopalians, and Elder Bates, of the Adventists. They found the Town Hall crowded with a curious and not very sympathetic assembly. It was evident that there were not a few of these auditors who were quite of the mind of the historic deacon: they were ready to be convinced, if they were in error, and would like to see the man that could do it. But the New Albion delegation had no misgivings. They knew that the idea they advocated was right and reasonable, and they talked like men who expected to carry their point. The speech of the evening, all things considered, was that of Mr. Hartwell. Several years of his earlier ministry had been spent in these small towns, and he spoke from a full experience of the evils of sectarian division.

"I never was in Monroeville before," he said; "but I have lived in towns just like it, and I can tell something about the state of things in this town which will be no news to you, but which it may do you no harm to hear. Your five little societies, living here at a poor, dying rate, do not have a very good time. You cannot live without help from outside; that is confessed. With all the help you can get, none of these churches is able to offer its pastor a decent living. The salaries are so small that the grade of men you are able to secure is extremely low. Now and then a man of good gifts and great fidelity, like the venerable pastor of the Baptist Church, settles in a town like this and stays many years; but the great majority are young men who will not stay more than a year or two, or men who have failed everywhere else, and who sometimes fasten themselves on you and give you plenty of trouble in getting rid of them. The Methodists have a way of managing such cases; but the Methodist churches in these small towns rarely keep a man through the three years that the discipline allows, unless he is a man they do not want. Is not that true?

"The consequence is that your Christian work is poorly done. Many waste places in the corners of these towns are sadly neglected, and are becoming rapidly heathenized. The religious wants of these communities are not so well provided for as they were in the days when there was but one church. You say that you are sending down to the cities a constant stream of your young men, and that is true; but the young men that you are sending us nowadays are not of so good a quality as those you sent fifty years ago. The young men of your town do not get so much benefit from your churches as they got fifty or sixty years ago. How can they? What have you here to attract the attention and command the respect of intelligent young men? Your feeble, half-alive churches, that struggle for existence and are afflicted with chronic debility, do not strongly appeal to the enthusiasm of young men.

"The social life of your town is marred by these hateful divisions. The people of each church are a little clique; there are not enough of them to make it lively when they get together; petty sectarian jealousies keep you apart. If the Methodists have a fair or a supper, very few go but their own folks; if the Congregationalists try to have a course of lectures, they must depend mainly on their own congregation for an audience. Of course, there is some denominational reciprocity, but it is limited. The barrenness of your social life is largely due to these sectarian divisions. They constitute one of the principal reasons why life here is undesirable — why people, especially young men, get away as soon as ever they can.

"So, then, even as things are now, with all the help you are getting, I am sure that you yourselves can see that you are not succeeding in doing for your town, with your present machinery, what needs to be done.

"The devotion and the earnestness of many men and women here is worthy of all praise; but the results of their work, as they will admit, are meager and unsatisfactory. If, then, things could go on upon the present basis, there would not be much encouragement in the prospect; but I am bound to tell you that I doubt whether things can go on much longer upon the present basis. I do not believe that the Christian people of the country will be willing much longer to contribute money for the perpetuation of these sectarian divisions. Many are beginning to see pretty clearly the foolishness and sin of them, and to demand that they shall cease. This is a fact to which you must give due heed. You are wise enough to make a virtue of necessity.

"Think, if you can, how much better it would be to have one religious society here instead of five. You could have one good church edifice; you could take the largest and best of your three and renovate and beautify it for your place of worship, and fit up one of the others for a lecture hall and for other social purposes. You could have one first-rate minister, and pay him a good salary, and not need to beg a cent of it from anybody. You could have your pick of all the singers in town for your choir. You would have one fine congregation,— large enough to make preaching and listening, too, much more inspiring. Your minister would be likely to remain with you several years,— long enough to get acquainted with the absentees of the out-districts, to gain their friendship, and to mature plans of successful work among them. Your social life would be improved. By combining all your forces, you could have singing schools, concerts, courses of lectures, reading circles, various literary and musical diversions of an excellent character. Monroeville would be a pleasanter place to live in; people would not be in such a hurry to get away; property would cease to depreciate.

"What is the condition of all this gain? Simply that you should drop your small, sectarian prejudices, and begin to be what the disciples were called at Antioch — Christians. nothing more nor less. Simply that you should learn to love Christ and His cause better than you love your own pet peculiarities of doctrine or worship. Is that impossible? Does anybody mean to say that the members of these churches in Monroeville are so narrow and obstinate that they cannot make so small a sacrifice for so great a good; that they will insist on maintaining in a town of eight hundred inhabitants five separate, starving, sectarian organizations instead of one vigorous, Christian church? Does any man tell me that the people of Monroeville, after coming together and looking this question in the face, are going away to say, 'It is of no use; we are too selfish and bigoted; we cannot live together peaceably; we must stick to our separate churches, though they perish, and religion and virtue and social life perish with them?' No, my friends. I have a better opinion of you. You have remained in this unhappy condition because you saw no good way out of it; now the way is open, and you will walk in it."

Mr. Hartwell's speech carried the day. A committee, consisting of the pastor and two members from each of the societies, was named on the spot and instructed to mature a plan of consolidation, to be presented to each of the churches. Within two months, all the old societies had been disbanded, and a new one formed under the style of Unity Church. The meeting-house of the Congregationalists, which was largest and most central, was retained as the house of worship; that of the Baptists was refitted as a social hall, and that of the Methodists was purchased by the town for a school-house,—the money thus obtained being devoted to a renovation of the other houses. The Apostles' Creed served the new church for its confession of faith, and its organization was in most respects similar to that of the church in Cyprusville. Mr. Slade easily found another field of labor in Kansas, the end of the conference year terminated Mr. Towne's stay in Monroeville, and Elder Crane, who continued to reside in the town, gratified the universal wish by taking charge of the new organization until a pastor could be found. The behavior of the good old clergyman in all this experience was eminently judicious and Christian. His rhetoric was turgid and his opinions were not modern, but his heart was sound and the people loved him.

Thus it was that five feeble bands of sectaries in one small town were united into one efficient and self-supporting Christian church.

XII.

A LITTLE more than two years after the Union mass-meeting in the Town Hall at Monroeville, on a delightful October evening, old Major stopped at the parsonage door, and the parson took his seat in the open buggy.

"Let's see; how long have you been gone?"

"Eighteen months, next Monday."

"And you've seen pretty much all that's worth seeing of Europe, Asia, and Africa?"

"Not quite, but enough to think of for some time."

"And you're thoroughly rested and well?"

"Never was so well in my life."

"Good! We were very anxious about you at first, but the later news comforted us. The people have taken solid enjoyment all the while in the knowledge that you were resting and recovering your health. They will give you a hearty welcome at the prayer-meeting to-morrow night."

"Bless their faithful hearts!" said the pastor, his eyes filling. "How gladly will I spend and be spent for them in the coming days! But tell me the news. I've had family news often, and church news now and then, but beyond these almost nothing. How goes the Club?"

"Gloriously! It is pushing right on to conquest. At every meeting we have news of some good fruit that has grown from its sowing."

"How fares the work among the poor?"

"We've got that into excellent shape. Mendicancy and pauperism are pretty effectually suppressed. There are no more beggars at our back doors; the tramps give us a wide berth. We hammered at the overseers of the poor till we got them to stop their careless largesses of alms to the idle and the vicious; they employ our visitors, now, to investigate their cases, and the amount of outdoor relief has been reduced sixty per cent."

"But I hope you haven't ended with suppressing pauperism?"

"Oh, no. Our visitors are beginning to take hold of the work of caring for the sick, and of helping the poor and the discouraged and the shiftless, in a most intelligent way. The work that has been accomplished, not only in ministering to the helpless, but in lifting up degraded families and inspiring the miserable with hopefulness and courage and self-respect, is the most genuine Christian work that has ever been done in New Albion."

" How about Dr. Strickland's kindergarten ? "

" There are three of them now, all doing excellently."

" The Young Men's Club — is that thriving ? "

" It has a membership of six hundred."

" And the County League — how is that flourishing ? "

" Now you begin to get down to business with your catechism. The County League, sir, has its foot upon its native hills, but its fame has gone into all the earth. Didn't you hear of it in Moab ? "

" Not a syllable," answered the parson, laughing.

" Well, sir, the Moabites may as well set their meeting-houses in order, for it will be after 'em shortly. See. You helped to reconstruct Monroeville. Scantico followed suit; but that was before you went away. Then the Outlook Committee got its eye on Rowell and began to put on a gentle pressure. The result there was different from that in the other two towns. The Methodist Church was pretty strong — much stronger than either of the other three, and the committee recommended elimination by subtraction instead of substitution. The Methodist Church kept its organization, but broadened its methods somewhat, and the other people gave up their own churches and went in with the Methodists. Of course, the Methodists did everything they could to make it agreeable for the others; put them into offices, got a quiet, broad-minded man for their next minister, and exercised a real Christian hospitality in their reception of the members of the other churches. I hear that they have all learned to sing the Jubilee song:

> "'A Methodist, Methodist will I live,
> And a Methodist will I die,'

with the spirit and the understanding also. That's Rowell. In Woodford, the Baptist Church was found to be the fittest to survive. The Baptist minister exchanges once a month regularly with the Rowell minister, and then the Baptists in Rowell who can't commune with the rest have a special communion service, and the Pedobaptists in Woodford who want their babies baptized have that service performed for them at their houses. In Tuckerton and Millville, union churches have been formed; and of the towns in this county where small populations were once split up among several feeble churches, all but two are now happy in the possession of one good church. Besides, our Outlook Committee has been spying out the neglected districts, and stirring up the people of the towns to occupy them; we have reports from them in the meetings of the County League, and I am sure that a great many more people in Bradford County are now under religious influences than there ever were before."

" Good !" shouted Mr. Strong.

" But you haven't got the whole of it yet," said Franklin. "To the next meeting of the County League, after you went away, a delegation of Dunham County folks, from Samsonville and Knox and other places, came in, and they got into the spirit of the movement, and went back and formed a Christian League in Dunham County. The matter began to be talked about all over the State. The newspapers took hold of it, and pushed it hard ; the business men perceived the reasonableness and justice of it, and made their influence felt in favor of it, and soon every county in the State had swung into line. Midland County was the last to organize, and their league was formed last April, five months ago. And week before last the secretaries and outlook committees of all the county leagues held a meeting in Bradford, and formed 'The Christian League of Connecticut.' Its object, as stated in the constitution, is 'to promote efficiency and economy in Christian work, by the suppression and extinction of superfluous organizations, by the occupation of destitute fields, and by the concentration of the efforts of Christian people.' We are to have one mass-meeting every year, in

November, to hear reports from the county secretaries, to read and discuss papers, and to devise measures for the prosecution of our work."

"*Laus Deo!*" exclaimed the parson. " Who would have believed it! Why, this is more of a miracle than your telephone, that has sprung into being since I went away. *Gloria in excelsis!* The unity of believers in this commonwealth is no longer merely a sentiment; it is a solid fact. Have they heard of this yet up in Massachusetts?"

"Oh, yes, they are talking about it there, and out West, too. The West, you know, is a great deal worse sect-ridden than we are, and sensible people out there are beginning to see that they must organize to protect themselves against the nuisance. A keen fellow from Dakota, a leading man in one of the churches out there, was in our bank the other day, talking it over. 'Your outlook committees may do very well for this region,' he said; 'what we've got to have is a vigilance committee. I go in for hanging every man that proposes the second church in a town of less than five hundred people. On one of our railroads, the other day, away out on the prairie, fifty miles from anywhere, the surveyor got off the train to stake out a new town. He drove four stakes and went away to eat his dinner by a spring, and, bless my soul! when he come back, there was a church extension agent a-sitting on every one o' those stakes — a Baptist on one and a Presbyterian on another and a Methodist on another and a Congregationalist on another. They'd all come to locate churches in the new town. That's about the way they do it,' said my friend, 'and they've got to stop it.'"

"That will pass, for Dakota," laughed Mr. Strong. "There are facts, no doubt, under your friend's hyperbole. But we will trust that something less sanguinary than a vigilance committee may serve to restrain the rampant sectarianism of the West."

"Ay, ay," cried the banker. "A little patience and sweet reasonableness, and a great deal of pluck and perseverance will do the business. Let people once see how much better and more Christian is coöperation than competition and conflict, in doing Christian work, and the battle is won."

"I always knew that the millennium was coming," said Mr. Strong, slowly, resting his eye for a moment on the mingled pearl and gold in the cloudless sky, out of which the sun had just sunk, and then dropping it to take in the soft, purple haze of the hills and the shining depths of the placid river; "I always knew that it was coming, but I never knew before just how it was coming. Now I see."

XIII.

IT was a bright afternoon in early November; the keen west wind was making a great stir among the tough brown leaves in the oak grove near by, and the prophecy of a sharp frost was in the air, while the Reverend Theodore Strong and his friend Walter Franklin walked briskly up and down the platform of the railway station at Potsdam Junction. They were waiting for the Southern Express, due in a few minutes, which was to carry them to Bradford.

"Is your programme ready?" asked the clergyman.

"Substantially," answered the banker. "The evening session is to be occupied by the address of Dr. Upson, followed by a social reunion in the parlors of the church."

"Upson presides, does he?"

"He does. Our rule is, you know, that the oldest pastor in the place where the convention is held shall take the chair at the meetings. This rule was adopted without thinking of the Methodists, but it doesn't work badly, after all. This is the third annual convention of the League, and Dr. Upson will be the second presiding officer furnished by the Methodists. It is his ninth year in Bradford—the third year of his second term with his present charge, and he served another church for three years between the two terms. So he happens to be the Bradford pastor longest in continuous service."

"I am glad of it," answered Mr. Strong. "He is a hearty and positive man; he believes in the League, and he will be sure to give us a breezy and stirring meeting. But what are we to have to-morrow?"

"Devotional hour from eight to nine; reports from county leagues, followed by conversation, for the forenoon session; two papers read and discussed at the afternoon session, and a public meeting in the evening, with three or four short speeches."

"This League gives you a great deal of work, old fellow; added to all of your other cares, it must burden you not a little. You must not let it make you its victim."

"Oh, no. This is my diversion. I like it better than a yacht or a stock-farm; it costs me less money and less worry than Thompson's fish-pond costs him—and that is his recreation, you know. Some of our directors laugh a little at my way of amusing myself, but the laugh is not always wholly on their side. I get about as much enjoyment out of my hobby as any of them gets out of his."

"I believe you," responded Mr. Strong, heartily. "I have often thought that business men might find in philanthropic enterprises of one sort or another not less diversion and more wholesome enjoyment than they derive from their various expensive relaxations. But there's the whistle."

In a few moments the train stopped at the junction. At the broad window of one of the palace cars sat a ruddy-faced gentleman, in a loose gray traveling suit, looking out at the group of passengers and gazers on the platform. His eye fell on the parson, and instantly he raised the window and shouted:

"Ho, there, my friend!"

Mr. Strong's eye was lifted to the window, and he answered the salutation by springing to the platform of the car. Franklin followed him The stranger met him at the door and greeted him warmly.

"Bless my soul!" he cried, "this is indeed an unexpected pleasure. I wondered much, on my way over, whether I should see you; but I had not your address, and did not know where to look for you in all this vast country. You remember how unexpected was our parting?"

"I remember well," replied the parson, heartily. "This meeting is just as unexpected, and far more welcome. But allow me to introduce my friend, Mr. Franklin. This is Mr. Thornton, an English gentleman with whom I journeyed from Acre to Damascus."

"And for whom," interrupted the stranger, "you so kindly cared when he was prostrated by the heat. I owe much to your friend, Mr. Franklin."

"So do many of us," answered the banker, sententiously.

"But when did you arrive on these shores?" asked the parson.

"The day before yesterday."

"Is it your first visit to America?"

"It is the first."

"And how far are you going on this train?"

"Only to Bradford. It is the next station, I believe."

"It is, and it is our destination also."

"Good!"

The Englishman paused a moment, and then said:

"I am on my way to a convention in that city of what is called the Christian League. You know of it, I dare say."

"Oh, yes; Mr. Franklin, here, is the father of it."

"Bless my soul! This is Mr. Walter Franklin! and you are the Rev. *Theodore* Strong! Well, well! I have often wondered, as I read in the English papers the doings of the club, whether my sometime-friend in Damascus could be the Mr. Strong of New Albion. The name was the same, but I hardly thought it the same man. This doubles the delight of the meeting. And you, sir," turning to Mr. Franklin, "are to be profoundly congratulated. The Christian League is a child of which a man has a right to be proud."

"Oh, that is Strong's extravagance," protested Franklin. "The Christian League, unlike the Corinthian Church, has many fathers. I am only serving it as a sort of dry nurse for the time being."

"We know all about that!" exclaimed the Englishman. "The history of the League is quite familiar to many on the other side of the sea. As good luck would have it, I saw the announcement of your convention in one of the New York newspapers yesterday, and at once resolved to be present. Are you the president of the League?"

"No; the League has no officers, save a business committee appointed at each meeting to make arrangements for the next. We pass no votes and keep no records. We meet simply for conference and discussion. I have served, thus far, as the secretary of the Business Committee; they have done me the honor to re-appoint me year by year; that is the only office I hold."

"And that," interposed Mr. Strong, "is no sinecure, as you may guess. The prosperity of the League is largely due to the abundant and gratuitous labors of my friend. That will be plain to you before the meeting is ended. But here we are at Bradford."

A delegation from the Bradford League was at the station to receive them, and the Englishman, protesting, was carried off by his friends to their lodgings.

At seven o'clock, when the three appeared at the door of the spacious social parlors of the Summerfield Methodist Church, where the meeting was to be held, they found some scores of gentlemen and ladies gathered in groups, and filling the room with the noise of conversation and laughter. Recognitions, greetings, introductions, showed that these were delegates to the convention, who had come from various parts of the State, who were not altogether unacquainted, and among whom it was easy to establish the bond of a cordial fellowship. Mr. Franklin and Mr. Strong were quickly surrounded and warmly welcomed. To extricate Mr. Thornton from the throng that pressed around them, Mr. Strong put him in charge of Mr. Stanley, rector of the Episcopal Church in Waterport, who was standing near.

"I myself am a Churchman," said the Englishman, as the two walked away to a quiet nook, "and the doings of this League have greatly interested me. There is need enough, in our country, of coöperation among Christians, and I have come to this meeting to see whether its methods would be at all practicable in England."

"I do not know how that would be," answered the rector; but I can think of no reason why they would not work with you as well as with us. 'Sweetness and light' are the only weapons of our warfare; if your arsenals are not full of these, one of your countrymen is not to blame. We disseminate information; we bring Christian people of all names together to talk about the work in which they are all engaged; we try to promote unity and good-will among them. Such methods as these ought to be feasible in England."

"They ought to be, indeed," replied Mr. Thornton; "but there are so many technical and formal difficulties. For example, there is the everlasting fuss about orders; how do you manage that?"

"We have nothing to do with orders," answered the clergyman. "There is no occasion whatever for raising any such question. Nobody takes orders and nobody gives orders. We do nothing in our clubs, nor in this League, as ministers or as churches. We meet simply as Christian neighbors to confer about our work and the best ways of promoting it."

"But your genuine High Churchman never could take part in any such conferences."

"I don't know about that. Of course, the High Churchman who really thinks that these religious societies of the Baptists and the Congregationalists and the Methodists are not only irregular but irreligious bodies, and that they ought to be resisted and extirpated, could not have anything to do with our League; but there are few High Churchmen, I fancy, who ever go as far as that. I myself am thought, by some of my brethren, to be a pretty rigid Churchman; but I am quite ready to admit that these other religious bodies are doing efficient Christian work; and when such an organization is occupying any field, preaching the Gospel to the people and helping them to lead pure and upright lives, I do not think that Churchmen are called to enter that field, to divide and scatter the forces there at work. It is far better for us to spend our strength on some destitute neighborhood. I cannot quite admit that these religious societies are genuine churches, or that their ministers are properly ordained; but what of that? You may call them what you will—conventicles or debating societies; the question is not what name they ought to bear, but what they are doing; and if your conventicle or your debating society is making men act like Christians, then I think we Churchmen had better not tear it into pieces, that we may build a 'regularly organized' church out of its ruins. There is better business for us, I am sure."

"Hear, hear!" responded Mr. Thornton.

"Well, that is all that this League stands for. It promotes comity and coöperation among Christians of different names. It asks me to do nothing more than Archbishop Tait, of Canterbury, the Primate of all England, has done more than once, as you know. He has repeatedly welcomed and invited conferences with dissenters, for the more effectual prosecution of religious work."

"You speak truth," assented the Englishman. "And I can see no reason why some such measures might not be adopted in my own country. Your League, as I understand it, is only a device for generating and guiding public sentiment."

"That is all; and this is done simply by bringing Christian people together, putting the facts before them, and inducing them to talk them over. But the bell is tolling for the evening service; let us find seats in the church."

Dr. Upson's opening address was a spirited and enthusiastic one, but there is no room for it in these chronicles. After the address, the reunion proceeded, the citizens of Bradford being present in force to welcome the delegates. It was delightful to witness the unconstrained and hearty manners of the company; nobody seemed to have a burden on his mind; there were no knots or slate-makers or wire-pullers; no one had a pet measure that he wanted to put through the convention on the next day; no one expected any office. In all these respects it was quite unlike the preliminary meetings of many ecclesiastical bodies; and to this difference was due in part, no doubt, the excellent temper of the members.

The morning prayer-meeting was almost wholly devotional. To singing and prayer, more than to speech-making, the hour was devoted; the old hymns that express the unity of the Church were sung with a wholesome fervor; the prayers laid hold upon the words of the Intercessor, "that they all may be one," as if they really expected that the answer would come.

Promptly, at the hour of nine, Mr. Franklin called the convention to order.

"We are hampered by no formalities," he said; "we are ready to proceed at once to business. According to our unwritten rule, the duty of presiding at this meeting falls to the Rev. Dr. Upson, in whose church we meet, and he will now take the chair."

"The Business Committee recommend," said the chairman, mounting the platform, "that the forenoon until half-past twelve be given to reports from the county committees and to conversation about them — fifteen minutes to each report, which may be oral or written; ten minutes to the discussion of it. Of course, there is no room for speeches; but some of you will want to ask questions of the persons reporting, for further explanation of portions of their report. We want you to get your questions into definite shape before you present them. A great many questions can be asked and answered in ten minutes, if no words are wasted. Brother Dickinson, you have the floor."

The secretary from Midland County, thus addressed, rose and began the reading of his report, which we summarize:

Of the twenty-nine towns and cities in the county, twenty-two have coöperated during the last year in the work of the County League. In all the large towns League clubs have been formed, and in the small towns the work of consolidation has been steadily advancing. The county contains a population of seventy thousand. Two years ago, there were one hundred and fourteen regularly organized churches in this county, besides various missions and congregations of a more or less ephemeral character. Of these churches, forty-one were in the cities and in the towns with over five thousand inhabitants; the remaining seventy-three were in the smaller towns. The large towns and cities contain about forty-five thousand people; the small towns about twenty-five thousand. In the large towns and cities there was about one church to every twelve hundred inhabitants; in the smaller towns there was about one to every three hundred and fifty inhabitants. Now, there are but ninety-three churches in the county, a reduction of twenty-one in the whole number. (Applause.) In the cities and large towns, four churches have been disbanded, none of which had any other than sectarian reasons for its existence, and eight new ones have been formed, making a gain of four churches in the denser populations. In the small towns, twenty-five churches have been disbanded and no new ones formed, so that in these sparser populations there is now about one church for every five hundred persons. (Applause.) Statistics, so far as procurable, indicate that, with the decrease in the number of churches, there has been an increase of from eight to ten per cent. in the number of regular worshipers, the movement toward consolidation having enlisted the interest of many persons who had previously remained outside of all churches, quite a number of them being men of intelligence and property, to whom the sectarian divisions had always been a stumbling-block.

In all the towns where churches were consolidated, a movement was at once set on foot to establish mission services in districts distant from the church, and these were generally well attended and useful; but several towns have settled upon a method which seems to be more successful. It is that of bringing the people to the central place of worship, instead of sending the Gospel to them. In the town of Summit, three four-horse teams, coming by different roads, bring to church every Sunday morning about fifty persons, none of whom had previously been in the habit of attending church. The teams are furnished by farmers in each neighborhood; the farm wagons have been provided with springs and comfortable seats, and the invitation has been extended to all the people living on the roads through which these conveyances pass to make use of them in going to church. Every house was visited, the poorest people were made to feel that they would be welcome, and in some cases aid was quietly given to families who found it difficult to provide their children with suitable clothing. The result is a great increase in the attendance at the church in the center of the town. Quite a number of the farmers who have conveyances of their own, but have never use'd them on Sunday, have been stirred up to attend church, and the four-horse teams are accompanied by a goodly number of smaller vehicles. The old horse-sheds in the rear of the meeting-house are filled every Sunday. This policy of concentration seems to be gaining in favor in Midland County. It is thought to work better than the plan of holding many small meetings in the separate neighborhoods. The school-houses are not always comfortable; the lights are dim, the singing drags, the attendance in each place is small. The central church, on the other hand, is commodious and cheerful; there is an organ or some other instrument, and a choir to lead the singing; and the greatly increased attendance doubles the interest and enthusiasm of the auditors, stimulates the preacher to do his best, and increases the moral effect of the whole service. Instead of distributing the broken meats of the Gospel-feast to the people in the out-districts, the people themselves are brought to the first table and enjoy the best that the house affords. This tends wonderfully to strengthen the feeling of community between different parts of the town, and to prevent local jealousies and feuds. It is pleasant and useful for the people of all parts of the town to meet thus once a week. Those who advocate this method point also to the fact that, in thus drawing the whole town together at one central place of worship, they are only restoring the practices of the earlier days, when these country towns were much more populous and prosperous than they now are.

Mr. Dickinson's report was received with a round of applause.

"Now for your questions!" cried the chairman. "The report has occupied only thirteen minutes; you have twelve minutes for talk. Stand up, Brother Dickinson! Go on, brethren!"

"Is there only one church in this town of Summit?"

"Only one. Five of our country towns have but one church apiece!"

"What kind of a church is it?" The question came from two or three parts of the room at the same time.

"It is called, I believe, 'The Church of Christ in Summit.'"

"Were there other churches in the town formerly?"

"Yes; there were three churches, two years ago."

"What has become of the buildings?"

"The Congregational Church stood in a breezy place on the top of the highest hill; it was bought and remodeled for a summer boarding-house. The Baptist Church is vacant. The Methodist Church, renovated, is the one now occupied."

"Is that old vacant Baptist church a pleasant object to look upon?" asked one elderly, quiet-faced man, who rose up under the gallery.

"No, it is not," answered Mr. Dickinson, with some feeling. "It is to me a very melancholy spectacle. Some of the shutters have been torn off, and many panes of glass have been broken from the windows. The thought of what it is likely to become fills me with pain. My boyhood was spent in Summit, and I was a worshiper in that old church. I do not like to see it falling into ruin."

"There is another such vacant church in our town," continued the old gentleman; "ours is a Congregational church, the church in which I used to worship when I was a boy; the church where I stood up to confess my faith; the church where my father served for many years as deacon, and from whose doors he was carried out to be buried. I am glad of the union which has brought the Christians of our town all together again as in the olden time; I praise God for it every day; I am perfectly at home in our new union church, which stands in the factory village; but the sight of that dear old church, falling into decay and desolation, is a perpetual sorrow to me. I know of three other towns in our county where the same melancholy spectacle may be seen. The movement toward consolidation leaves on many of our hills dear and venerable churches to be hiding-places for the moles and the bats, and sometimes for worse vermin. Forgive me for speaking so long, but I want to raise this question: What should be done with vacant churches?"

The responses from all parts of the room showed that the question had touched the hearts of the delegates. There was a short pause. Finally, the chairman spoke:

"What answer do we hear from Midland County?"

"It is a question on which I myself wish to be enlightened," answered Mr. Dickinson.

"If the convention will permit me to prophesy," said the chairman, "I will venture the prediction that the report from Dunham County will deal with this subject. It may be well to wait for that. Indeed, the twelve minutes are all gone but one, and I propose that we devote that minute to singing the verse:

"I love thy Church, O God!
Her walls before thee stand,
Dear as the apple of thine eye,
And graven on thine hand."

XIV.

AFTER the singing of this stanza with deep feeling, Mr. Hubbard, the secretary of the Dunham County League, began his report. The result had been somewhat less favorable than those contained in the preceding report, but there was still abundant reason for encouragement in the reduction of the number of small churches, in the great increase of church attendance, and in the effectiveness of the new methods of reaching the churchless classes. That part of Mr. Hubbard's report to which the chairman referred, we reproduce entire:

"We have had troubles of our own with vacant churches; troubles not merely sentimental, but practical. The consolidation in the town of Liberty left the Methodist Church vacant; and it was not only an offense to the eyes and a trouble to the heart, as every vacant church must be, but it became the haunt of tramps, and was a scandal to the community. At length, the good people determined to abate the nuisance in some way, and a meeting of the citizens was called in the old church itself, one evening last August, to consider what should be done with it. Among those who came to the meeting were several city people who were spending the summer in Liberty, some of whom were natives of the town. Various uses of the old sanctuary were suggested. One of the farmers offered one hundred dollars for it, to be used as a barn; but the offer was not entertained. One heroic brother wanted to burn it up at once; it had outlived its usefulness, he said, and might better be solemnly devoted to God as a burnt offering than to live to be a disgrace and a pest to the community. This proposition pleased some of the more enthusiastic Christians and all the boys, and it was on the point of being adopted, when Judge Forsyth, of New York, arose and made a little speech.

"'It seems to me,' he said, 'that you can put this church to a better use. I do not like to see valuable property destroyed, and I have personal reasons for not wishing that the church in which I worshiped when a boy should come to such an end. You need a parsonage and parish house, a home for your minister and a social center for the community. This building can be remodeled at no great cost, so that it shall serve this double purpose. I have had my friend Mr. Garland, the architect, who is here to-night, make a plan for this reconstruction, which he will show you. The walls of the building are high enough to admit of two stories; the two rows of windows lend themselves to the plan; a floor can be thrown across, at about the height of the gallery floor; the lower story can be divided into rooms suitable for the parsonage; above, you can have your parish hall, for lectures, concerts, sociables, literary meetings, etc., with a room for the library which I hope you will have by and by, and of which your pastor should have the care. Mr. Garland tells me that the change in the building can be made according to his plan for about fifteen hundred dollars; and I am prepared to say that if the community will pledge five hundred dollars of that amount, I will furnish the rest.'

"The offer of Judge Forsyth was received with loud applause; the five hundred dollars was pledged at once, the carpenters were soon at work, and the pastor is now living in his parsonage, while the parish is rejoicing in such a place of social assembly as every country parish needs. I have heard that some other wealthy gentlemen, natives of Liberty, now residing in Boston, are proposing to endow the library at which Judge Forsyth hinted, and for which a room was provided in the reconstructed building.

"Thus one of our old churches has been converted and saved from ruin in its old age. But there was more serious trouble in Hector. There it was the old Baptist Church that was abandoned, and the kind of tramps that it harbored were mostly religious tramps. Unluckily there were a few members of that church who proved incorrigible when the union was formed; they opposed it to the end, and in the face of an overwhelming public sentiment they continued to oppose it after it was an accomplished fact. These irreconcilables were determined to keep up some kind of sectarian division in the community, and they used the old church as their base of operations. The same tactics have been resorted to in other towns. A vacant church acts on the mind of your religious demagogue as a powerful stimulant. He wants to use it for schismatic purposes. He cannot rest till he has gathered his awkward and ugly squad of sectaries within its walls. Very likely, too, he will name his schism shop a 'Union Church.' Many an enterprise of this nature, whose only effect could be to divide and weaken the Christian community, has been baptized with the Union name. So it was in Hector. First a traveling Baptist minister came along and held 'Union' services in the old church for a few weeks; but it was not long before he discerned the true character of his supporters and turned his back upon them.

Their next resort was a Congregationalist from Bradford, who goeth about as a roaring layman, seeking whom he may exhort. His excuse for invading Hector was the lack of orthodoxy in the pulpit of the village church, and he began his campaign by attacking the 'loose doctrines' and the heretical tendencies of the pastor. But a lawyer of Hector, who had some knowledge of this heresy hunter's business operations, made a brief statement in the county newspaper, and the fellow had the grace to take himself off. After him came a band of Adventists, with a series of meetings, and after them an itinerant Universalist, who tried to get up a discussion of his peculiar doctrines, and challenged the pastor to a controversy; but the night after his first meeting — a cold, winter night — the stove was left open, a spark set it on fire, and the old church was saved from being the kennel of schismatics, yet so as by fire. But the fate of this and other vacant churches in our county has warned us against leaving in our rear, as we march toward Christian union, such a fortress of schism as a vacant church may become. Henceforth we are determined to find some good use for every church that is vacated; it might far better be devoted to secular uses than be left to become a sanctuary for the bats or a den for tramps or religious demagogues."

After Mr. Hubbard's report was concluded, a delegate rose and asked, timidly:

"May I tell what we did with our two old churches?"

"Certainly," answered the chairman.

"We sold them."

"For what uses?" inquired half a dozen at once.

"One was bought by the town for a school, the other by a physician for a sanitarium and boarding-house."

"How much did you get for them?" demanded some speculative disciple.

"Five thousand dollars for the two."

"What did you do with the money?" came in several voices.

"We invested it in a fund for the benefit of the church."

"How long ago was that?" It was Mr. Franklin who asked this question.

"Two years ago last spring."

"So you have had the benefit of this fund now two years. How do you thrive under it?" continued Mr. Franklin.

"At first, we thought ourselves very rich; but when we came to figure up our income, we found that it had fallen off considerably. The year before, we had raised fifteen hundred dollars with no difficulty; the interest on our fund reduced the amount about three hundred dollars, but it was twice as hard to raise twelve hundred dollars that year as it had been to raise fifteen hundred the year before. A good share of our parishioners fell back upon that fund and shut up their purses with a snap, and would not give anything. Last year, it was still worse; we began to be afraid that we should not be able to raise a thousand dollars. Finally, we called a meeting and determined to get rid of that millstone. By a vote of two to one we turned the money over to the town to be used in endowing a free library, and then we sang the doxology."

Laughter and cheers greeted this illuminating speech.

"He that hath ears to hear, let him hear!" cries Dr. Upson. "A bank vault is a poor place for a church of Christ to lay up its treasure in. We will now hear from Ridgefield County. Brother Harlan, you have the floor."

It was evident that Brother Harlan was a character. A man in plain farmer's clothes, with keen gray eyes glancing out from beneath beetling brows, a shock of refractory red hair, and a close-cropped beard of the same color, ambled to the front and began deliberately:

"I'm not the secretary of our county," he said. "Captain Thomas is sick, and he sent word to me day before yesterday that I must come here and report for him. I haven't a word written, and I shall not begin to tell all that ought to be told about the work in our county; but I'll give a few facts that have come under my own eye. I don't know much about the figures, but I know that quite a lot of sickly churches have been killed off. And that's the right way to serve 'em. We thin out a hill o' corn that has seven or eight stalks when there isn't room for more than three or four, and get a better crop for doin' it. When churches come up too thick around here on these hills, they've got to be thinned out in the same way. Poor husbandry, I calc'late, to keep diggin' round 'em and manurin' 'em with home missionary money, when there's no more chance of gettin' a crop from 'em than there is from a patch o' corn that's sowed broadcast.

"In the town where I live, in Ridgefield County, we had three churches for more'n twenty years. Fifty years ago there wasn't but one, and the population was fifty per cent. larger then than it is now. Two years ago, the Congregationalists and the Methodists made up their minds to come together; they kept both meetin' houses, and the united society worships in one in the mornin' and in the other in the evenin', and that accommodates both ends of the street. We have a congregation a good deal larger than the two put together used to be, and we pay our minister, easy enough, a good, comfortable salary. The fact is, we've got a minister that it's easy enough to pay. He's a keen-witted, level-headed young man who understands himself and his business, and knows something outside of his business, too. Everybody likes him. He talks to us very plain in church; it comes right from his heart; and when he is around among the farmers he don't find it hard to make talk come. He knows his Bible and he knows other books; but he knows men, too, and cattle and sheep and horses,—especially horses. He's got one of the likeliest colts in town, and he keeps his coat as shiny as satin. The other day, the parson was sittin' in his buggy in front of one of the stores, talking with half a dozen men, when along came old Sime Harrison, who lives up at Scrabbletown. Sime's one of those terrible slovenly critters that keeps everything at loose ends around his farm, is always behindhand with his work, and never pays his debts; but because he is so loose in everything else, he tries to even things up by being mortal strict in his religious notions. He generally drives his horses tandem, because he never gets ready to rig a whiffletree and a pole. It's a city fashion, I understand; but we farmers consider it a dreadfully shiftless way to hitch up horses. So Sime comes a drivin' up his two old nags afore his buckboard, and he stops when he gets opposite the parson, and leanin' over toward him in a kind o' confidential way, he says: 'Brother Hall, do you think the 'Postle Paul ever druv a fast hoss?' 'Don't know about that,' answers the parson, quicker'n lightnin', 'but I'm pretty sure he never drove two horses tandem.' You'd ought to have heard them men shout. Sime didn't want to know any more about the 'Postle Paul, and he druv right on. But that's the sort o' man our minister is. Smart as a whip, I can tell you! He stands square on his feet, looks you right in the eye, and commands the respect of everybody. It's a great thing for the town, and especially for our boys who are growin' up, to have a man like that around among us,—a gentleman, a scholar, a man of sense and self-respect, a man who pays his debts, and has no need to beg of anybody or to be beholden to anybody for his livin'. It makes religion seem a sensible and respectable sort of thing.

"One Sunday evenin' last spring, we had a Sunday-school concert, and our pastor went down to the West village to preach to them, because they hadn't any minister. The next day I was down there, and everybody was talkin' about his sermon. 'Made it jest as plain as daylight,' they said. 'Can't help listenin' to him.' 'Understood every word he said.' 'Wish

I could hear such preachin' every Sunday,' says Deacon Chapin. 'Well, what's to hinder you hearin' it?' says I. 'What do you mean?' says he. 'I'll tell you what I mean,' says I. 'It's two mile and a half to the old church in the East village. When I was a boy I lived half a mile further west than you do, and our folks was always at the old church every Sunday, rain or shine, and so was quite a number of families livin' down this way. It isn't any further now'n was then, and there's better roads.'

"'But there's a good many families in this neighborhood that haven't teams,' he said.

"'Well, then, git up one or two gig-teams and bring 'em.'

"'It'd cost too much.'

"'Would it? How much does it cost you a year to keep your church goin'?'

"'Well, about six hundred dollars is the least.'

"'And how many do you git to church?'

"'Forty or fifty, ginerally.'

"'Yes; and a good share of them has teams of their own. Now you can arrange for teams that wont cost you more'n five dollars a Sunday, that'll take at least thirty persons up to the old church. I'm an old stager, and I'd like to take the contract of transportin' thirty from the West village to the East village and back ag'in every

Sunday for five dollars. The rest can go with their own teams. You wont want to get your preachin' for nothin' up there, of course; but you can pay for that and pay the expense of transportation, and then save money on what it costs you to keep up this church. Besides, you can have first-class preachin' every Sunday, instead of four hundred and forty-fourth class.'

"'But there will be many Sundays,' said the Deacon, 'that it will be stormy, or the roads would be bad and we couldn't go so far.'

"'There might be five or six Sundays every year,' I answered, 'when the roads would be bad. But how many Sundays in a year on the average are you out of preachin' on account of a vacancy in your pulpit?'

"The Deacon looked over the church books and found that for the last five years the pulpit of the church in the West village had been without a supply fifty-five Sundays in all—just eleven Sundays a year on the average. He agreed with me right off that there would not be so many Sundays as that in the year when the roads between the two villages would be too heavy for travelin'. And the result of our talk was that a meetin' of the people in the West village was held, the matter was talked up, a subscription to pay for teams was started, and now we bring the West villagers to church and Sunday-school at the East village every Sunday, and git more of 'em than ever went to their own church. They keep up their own Sunday-school, too, in the afternoon, and their prayer-meetin' in the evenin', but they like the present arrangement, and wouldn't on any account go back to the old plan.

"In several other towns of our county the same thing, or something very much like it, has been done. We have seen the tribes that have been scattered abroad return with singin' unto Zion. We aint exactly *standin'* in the old ways, as the prophet says, but we're walkin' in 'em, or, rather, drivin' over 'em up to Jerusalem; and it seems good to have the people of the whole town come together with one accord in one place, just as they did on the day of Pentecost. We've had some Pentecosts of our own, too, in Ridgefield County, and I should like mightily to tell you all about 'em; but I've kept my eye on the clock, and know that my time's up."

Brother Harlan's shrewd harangue was received with much laughter and applause, and as soon as it was ended the questions began.

"How large is your congregation on Sunday morning?"

"Last Sunday I counted three hundred and eighty-nine. It was not above the average."

"That is a large congregation," interposes

Dr. Upson. "Few of those in the cities are so large."

"How many do you think would have been found in the three churches on a pleasant Sunday, before the consolidation?"

"Not above three hundred."

"Is your church entirely self-supporting?"

"*Yes*, sir."

"Do your people contribute to any missionary or benevolent societies?"

"Last year we gave over three hundred dollars."

"How do you manage that?"

"We take a collection every month. Several of these collections are for Union societies. When we take up our collection for foreign missions or home missions, or the publication cause, we distribute envelopes in the pews, and each person puts his amount into an envelope, and writes on it the name of the society to which he wants it to go. If he is a Congregationalist, he sends his foreign missionary money to the American Board; if he is a Methodist, he sends it to the Methodist Board of Missions, and so on. The treasurer gathers up the amounts and forwards them to the right places, and reports to the church the amount of the collection and the sum remitted to each of the societies. At our monthly missionary meeting, we hear from the missions of all the denominations, and know a great deal more about what is going on in the mission field than we used to know when we heard only from the societies of one denomination."

"How do your contributions in envelopes compare with those in cash?"

"They're twice as big; partly because there's a little strife to see which society shall get the most, and partly because folks don't like to put a cent into an envelope."

Brother Harlan stepped down from the platform amid applause and a buzz of jocose comment. His report, informal and jocose as it was, had contained more meat than any that preceded it.

XV.

THE next to take the floor was Mr. Greene, the secretary from Bradford County. In this county are several cities and large towns, and the report was expected to deal not only with the problem of consolidating the small churches, but also with the important question of evangelization and charity presented by the urban populations. Bradford County contains New Albion, and was the home of the Christian League. Concerning the beginnings of the Union movement in some of the towns of this county, the readers of this history are fully informed.

In three of these towns, Mr. Greene's report showed that serious difficulties had been encountered. In Scantico, a few strenuous Methodists, egged on, as some said, by the presiding elder of the district, determined, after the Union church had been in successful operation for about a year, to reëstablish sectarian worship. Accordingly they demanded, in the name of the Methodist

Conference, the meeting-house which had formerly belonged to them, and which had been occupied for evening services by the united church. They asked for a minister; and a Methodist clergyman, partly disabled by ill-health, who was sojourning for the year in Bradford, was sent over to supply their pulpit. Unfortunately for their purposes, this clergyman was a man of broad views and generous temper, and he soon discovered the state of the public mind in Scantico. He called upon the pastor of the united church and proposed Union services in the Methodist Church in the evening, and in the other church in the morning, so that things went on for a few weeks much as before, the only difference being that there were two ministers instead of one. This was not exactly what his supporters had bargained for, but he was a man of so much intelligence and strength of character that they did not like to quarrel with him; and besides, it was somewhat ungracious to object to Union meetings. At length, he told the united congregation, one Sunday evening, that his work among them was finished, and that he should return the next day to Bradford; that Scantico needed but one church, and that one minister was better than two; that his brother Thomas, of the Union church, was a good enough Methodist for him; that he should file with the presiding elder his protest against the reëstablishment of Methodist worship in Scantico, and, if it became necessary, should carry the matter before the Conference at its next session; that the Methodist Church should not be made, if he could help it, an instrument for creating or perpetuating destructive schisms in the Church of Christ. This bold movement completely discomfited the Methodist sectarians, and they abandoned their scheme without a struggle.

In Tuckerton, it was a Congregational clique that made the trouble. In that town there had been two Congregational churches, the division arising out of a feud about a choir, and continuing for many years, until the Union church was formed. The Second Congregational Church stood in a small settlement dubbed by the Central villagers Potluck, in revenge for which the Potluckians persisted in applying to Tuckerton proper the contemptuous sobriquet of Kittleville. Much local warfare, of a nature not very sanguinary, had been waged between these two precincts from time immemorial, and it was considered a sure sign of the millennium when they agreed to come together and form a Union church. But this millennium did not last a thousand years, probably because the devil was not chained. He made his appearance in Potluck in the form of a Congregational minister of dubious credentials, who proposed to hold services in the church in that place, and by his unction and plausible speech contrived to deceive even the elect. To the ultra orthodox he suggested the danger of allowing their children to be trained up without any knowledge of the "doctrines of the fathers"; to those in whose breasts local pride burned most fiercely, he urged the ignominy of allowing Potluck to become "a mere suburb of Kittleville." Plying both these arguments industriously, he soon had quite a following at his heels, and almost before any one knew of it services were in full blast again in the Second Congregational Church. But a letter was written to some of the leading Congregationalists in Bradford and New Albion, and a strong delegation from the League clubs of those cities went down to Potluck, called together the leading Congregationalists of that precinct, assured them that they would fail of obtaining the Home Missionary aid on which they had depended for the support of their separate service, showed them the folly of the course into which they had been led, gave them some bits of the history of the man who had wormed himself into their confidence, and succeeded in bringing back Potluck from its wanderings, and in repairing once more the breach in the walls of the Tuckerton Zion.

In several other towns where Union movements had been set on foot, there had been outbreaks of a sectarian nature, some of which had not yet been subdued. The spirit of sect, like the Judaizing temper among the early Christians, was continually showing itself: men who had been bred in an intense sectarianism, who had been taught from their cradles to put the interests of sect above the interests of Christianity, could not all at once quench their unholy zeal and stop seeking, *first*, the kingdom of Methodism, or of Episcopacy, or of Congregationalism, and *its* righteousness; nevertheless, the broader sentiment and wiser methods of a genuine Christianity were all the while gaining strength, and the partisans of a narrow ecclesiasticism knew that they were fighting a losing battle. In quelling these sectarian outbreaks, the County League had been of the greatest service. Whenever any attempt had been made to form a new church or revive an old one in a town where the churches had been consolidated, the Outlook Committee, consisting of a representative of each of the denominations, had proceeded immediately to the spot, and had made a full examination of the circumstances, publishing the facts in the principal newspapers of the county, and making full reports of them at the next meeting of the League. These temperate but truthful representations generally brought a considerable pressure of public opinion to bear at once upon the offending schismatics; if that did not suffice, a committee, composed wholly of members of the sect to which they belonged, appointed by the County League at its next meeting to remonstrate with them and bring them to a better mind, sometimes had the desired effect. At all events, this County League, formed in the interests of Christian coöperation, concentrating and expressing all the most Christian sentiment of the county, keeping the eyes of its Outlook Committee on all the places where admonition or encouragement was needed, and swift to drag into the light of day all the hidden things of darkness that the spirit of sect lay in wait to do, was a mighty help in promoting the unity of believers and in preventing the reactions that were in danger of occurring here and there.

Mr. Greene's report, thus summarized, was given extemporaneously, and, like many another layman, he used up his time before finishing what he had to say. In the midst of his speech he was interrupted by the chairman:

"Time's up, Brother Greene. I know what you have left unsaid, and how important it is that you have a chance to say it. Perhaps it may be brought out in the conversation. Let me suggest to the convention that questions be asked about Christian League work in Bradford."

"That is just what I want to hear," spoke up Mr. Strong. "I know something about it, but I want to know more definitely. Will Mr. Greene tell us something of the charitable work of Bradford?"

"Thank you!" was the answer of the secretary. "I should have greatly failed of my duty if I had not brought something before the convention respecting this work. Our Charity Organization is an enterprise of the greatest importance, and it is the child of the Christian League Club of Bradford."

"What is the Christian League Club of Bradford?" asked Mr. Strong.

"It consists of the minister and one layman from each of the Protestant churches in the city. The organization is similar to that in New Albion, except that we have fewer laymen. With three laymen from each church, our club would be unwieldy."

"Go on with your story."

"When the club first faced the problem of poverty and pauperism, it found five charitable societies at work in the city, rivals and competitors, all striving to see which could 'relieve' the largest number of paupers, and collect and disburse the most money. Of course, they disbursed a deal of money, and of course pauperism was rapidly increasing. To secure coöperation among them seemed a hopeless task. At length, the club determined to solve the difficulty by organizing another society, which should be pledged to give no material aid whatever, but to work wholly by moral and industrial methods. A system of registration was adopted, by which the names of all persons receiving charity were recorded, with such information as could be gathered concerning each of them. The other societies and their churches were all invited to send to this bureau the names of all the persons relieved by them; and although this was at first refused by some of them, the measure was so evidently necessary for the exposure of imposture that they were obliged to adopt it. Immediately, we were able to notify the societies and the churches of many cases in which the same persons were receiving aid from two or more of them at the same time; and they soon found out the value of the bureau of registration. Then we divided the whole city into small districts, and after much labor succeeded in securing a competent visitor for each of these districts — one hundred and forty-seven in all. The charitable societies and the churches had had but few visitors — not a score of them in all the city. With all the money disbursed yearly, very little personal care and help had been bestowed on the poor, and this was the defect we sought to supply. We published a map of the city, with the districts numbered and the name of the visitor for each district, and offered the services of our visitors to the charitable societies and the churches for the investigation and care of the cases which they were called upon to relieve. Some intelligence and conscience in the administration of charity had begun to be developed, and the dispensers of charity readily availed themselves of our offer. Our visitors soon had their hands and hearts full. They were forbidden to give money or food or coal in any case, and were enjoined never to recommend the granting of such relief by the other societies, except in cases of sickness and absolute disability. Their problem was to help the poor without giving them money or subsistence; to help them by finding work for them, by rousing them to help themselves, by directing them into more frugal and comfortable habits of living, and by befriending them in every possible way. Our visitors were taught that this work of moral aid was, in the deepest sense of the word, a missionary work; that it could not be rightly done unless it was inspired by a 'genuine enthusiasm of humanity'; that it needed for its accomplishment a Christly sympathy and tenderness and tact, and a Christly courage and patience. Once in two weeks we have a meeting of all our visitors,— a conference meeting, in which each one has the privilege of giving his or her experience (they are mostly women), and of asking counsel about any hard cases. I tell you, brethren, these are the most interesting meetings I ever attended in my life. It would stir your hearts to listen to the stories told, and to see with what dauntless courage and what untiring patience and what marvelous tact and tenderness these good women are working for the salvation of the forlorn, discouraged, helpless creatures that are placed in their care. Our system does not allow a single visitor to have the care of more than two families at once; we do not believe that one visitor can, as a rule, do justice to more than two families; we want them to give to each family a great deal of time and care and personal attention; and the results of this patient, loving, hand-to-hand work among the poor of our city are full of encouragement."

"Don't you find some cases that are past saving?" some one inquired.

"We never admit it," was the answer. "There are cases in which, so far as we can see, no permanent improvement is made; but if 'men ought always to pray and not to faint,' then they ought always to work for those for whom they pray, and not to faint in their endeavors any more than in their prayers. I always remember what Robert Falconer said to his father, the wretched old drunkard, 'Father, you've *got* to reform some time, and you may as well begin now.' That is the substance of what he said. If we had a little more of that sort of purpose, we should save more of the hard cases."

"How many families have you cared for during the last year?"

"More than three hundred."

"What has been the effect upon the disbursements of the charitable societies?"

"They have been reduced about fifty per cent., and everybody admits that there is less suffering now than there was when the larger sum was distributed."

"What is the effect upon the morals of the city?"

"The sentences for drunkenness and petty crimes were fewer by fifteen per cent. last year than during the previous year."

"Do you attribute all this to the improved method of charity?"

"No; that would not be fair. Other important agencies have contributed to this result. To the establishment of friendly inns, quite as much is due."

"Tell us about them," came in half a dozen voices.

"My time is up."

"Mr. Greene may have ten minutes of my time," said the secretary from Rockbridge County. "My report will be largely a repetition of what we have heard already. This is more important."

The generous proposition was hailed with applause by the convention. Mr. Greene went on:

"Our club found, in fighting the saloons, that it was good tactics to borrow some of their weapons. We were confronted by exactly the same state of things as that which was discovered at New Albion, only our city is much larger than New Albion, and therefore the perils were greater and the needs more urgent. A large part of our population is without homes. The clerks, the operators in our manufacturing establishments, and the mechanics, are largely homeless. Such lodgings as most of them can afford are cold in winter and cheerless in all seasons; it is for warmth, shelter, and companionship, more than for drink, that many of them resort to the saloons. Some of them will go to the reading-rooms, but many, and those who are in greatest peril, have no taste for reading. The problem was to provide safe places of resort for this class of persons. We thought of a Young Men's Club, like that of New Albion; but it seemed advisable, as our territory is so large, to have several places of this character in different parts of the city. Accordingly, the plan of establishing friendly inns, or coffee-houses, in suitable localities, was suggested, and a company was incorporated, with a capital of ten thousand dollars, to prosecute this enterprise. It was not designed to be a charity; it was intended that the business should pay expenses from the start. The money was invested in lease and fixtures. Four suites of rooms, in different quarters of the city, were procured and fitted with counters, tables, crockery, cooking ranges, and furniture, and comfortable chairs; the intention was that they should be used for lunch-rooms during the middle of the day, and for places of resort in the evening. Many merchants and professional men, and some mechanics, it was thought, would take their midday lunch in these clean and comfortable places. The tables were to be partly removed in the evening, to give room for free movement and sociability. In each of the rooms an open fire was to be kept in the winter, and a fountain surrounded with flowers to cool and sweeten the air in the summer. Coffee, tea, chocolate, and milk were to be always on sale, with plenty of the nicest bakery rolls, biscuits, and the like; and in the summer, lemonade and soda-water with syrups of the best quality, at reasonable prices. A cup of coffee with rolls was to cost but five cents; a glass of milk but three cents. Newspapers were to be furnished, and various games, such as checkers, chess, and backgammon, were to be provided. It was thought best to make a small charge for the use of the games,—five cents for each person; and to avoid, so far as possible, every semblance of gambling practices, persons taking the games were required to pay for them in advance. In the rear of the large room, thus devoted to social purposes, was a smoking-room, well ventilated, with cozy chairs, where smokers could take their fill of their peculiar pleasure without encroaching upon the enjoyment of those to whom smoke is not delectable.

"After some such general plan as this, our coffee-rooms were all fitted up, the treasurer of the company giving much time and care to their arrangement. It is not too much to say that there are no saloons in Bradford half so pretty as they are. And it was believed that rooms so furnished could be rented to men who would pay the rent and a fair rate of interest on the capital invested. The problem was, of course, to find the right men; but there was no lack of applicants for the places, and the selections seem to have been wisely made. The inns have all paid expenses, and the stockholders have received a four per cent. dividend at the end of the first year. This success is due, largely, to the energy and business tact of the treasurer,

Mr. Marble, who has taken this for his diversion, and has found unbounded satisfaction in the working out of his plans. The belief that the opening of cozy, free-and-easy places of refreshment and social resort would draw many young men away from the liquor saloons has been abundantly justified by our experience."

"Why do you charge for the games?" asked some one.

"For revenue only," answered Mr. Greene. "We thought that habitués would be willing to pay a small price for their use, and that they might feel a little more comfortable about using them if they paid for them. There has been no complaint about the charge, and the amount received from this source nearly pays the rent of the building."

"Does your company keep any control of the rooms?"

"No; each friendly inn is under the control of its own landlord. We make a definite contract with him as to the kinds of refreshment he is to provide and the prices he is to charge, and the general regulations of the rooms; and, of course, we visit the inns frequently to see that they are properly kept and that the food and drink are of the best quality."

"Do you think that this has had any marked effect in reducing the amount of drunkenness?"

"I have no doubt that the great reduction shown by our police reports in the amount of drunkenness during the past year is largely due to the friendly inns."

As Mr. Greene was stepping down from the platform, amid the applause of the convention, Mr. Strong interrupted him:

"You have two minutes more. Are there not some other features of your charitable work in Bradford of which you ought to tell us?"

"I should be glad," answered the Bradford secretary, laughing, "to take twenty minutes more and tell you about our Employment Agency, our Industrial School, our Kindergartens, and our Day Nursery, all of which have sprung up in connection with our Charity Organization society, and all of which are important departments of its work. But I have talked too long already; if any one wants to know more about these forms of our Christian League work, I will show them to you this afternoon. They will speak best for themselves."

For the reports of the other county secretaries, there is no room in these chronicles. In many of their features they were similar to those already presented. They filled the morning session, and the interest had not flagged when the hour for adjournment came.

XVI.

THE afternoon session, according to the announcement, was devoted to the reading of two carefully prepared papers: the one by the Reverend Dr. Smalls, of New Liverpool, on "The True Definition of the Church," in which he defended the proposition that the Church consists of all the faithful people residing in any given community — that there is but one Church in any city or town, though there may be many congregations, worshiping in different places by different forms, and that the different congregations ought to recognize themselves as one Church and behave themselves accordingly. The other paper, read by Thomas Marshall, Esq., of Northbridge, on "Temperance and Tenement Houses," proved to be a most luminous exposition of the effects of unsanitary dwellings upon the drinking habits of the people, together with accounts of some of the recent experiments made by capitalists in the erection of improved tenement houses, well lighted, ventilated, and drained, and of the obvious effects upon the morals of their occupants. But as these papers were printed in full in the Bradford "Courier" of the next day, and must still be easily procurable, there is no need to reproduce them here.

For the same reason, it is unnecessary to report the two short speeches of the evening session. One matter, however, of deepest interest, must not be passed by. After the second speaker had taken his seat, Dr. Upson rose :

"I am sorry," he began, "to announce to this convention the only failure on our programme. Dr. Jackson, of Winchester, who was to make the closing speech, sends us a dispatch, which was received since the afternoon session, informing us that a railway accident on the Western road will prevent him from keeping his engagement. You will regret that as much as I do. But there are always compensations for our losses, if we know where to look for them ; and I think that I am on the track of one. The secretary of our Executive Committee, Mr. Walter Franklin—(applause)—has been receiving a good many letters from distant places, making inquiries about the working of the League, and giving information of movements that have been set on foot in other States with the view of carrying out its principles. I am sure that he could give us, if he would, some interesting and cheering reports. I have besought him to do so, but he has not consented; I am going now to pass him over to you, and let you deal with him as seems good to you."

The convention expressed its will in such a way that Mr. Franklin could not easily resist. He ascended the platform, amid a storm of cheers.

"Perhaps I ought to beg your pardon," he said, "for hesitating to bring you such tidings as I have; my only reason is my strong aversion to the sound of my own voice in a public place. But there are, as Dr. Upson has told you, quite a number of letters and newspaper clippings in my portfolio, showing the wide interest taken in our work, of which I will try to tell you something.

"The most amusing letters I receive are from persons who profess to be greatly interested in the history of our League, and who think the plan a beautiful one, but who fear that it is not practicable. There is no conservative so entertaining as your conservative who disputes an accomplished fact. You know that Dr. Dionysius Lardner proved, scientifically, that no vessel could be moved across the ocean by steam-power after the thing had been done. You know that an eminent electrician demolished the project of submarine telegraphy after messages had crossed the sea. And in like manner the measure of coöperation in Christian work proposed in the organization of the Christian League is demonstrated to be impracticable by a theorist here and there, long after the thing has been successfully worked out in many places. I will not trouble you with reading any of these letters; I have stuck them on pins to be preserved in my museum; about fifty years from now they will be highly interesting reading.

"Very amusing, also, are the letters from mystified correspondents, who wish to know whether there is a veritable Christian League in Connecticut. If they could only look into this crowded room and hear the noise you make, they would probably be convinced that the League is not a myth.

"The reports that come to us from all parts of the country show that the ideas of our League are taking hold of the people, especially of the laity, everywhere. I cannot begin to give you any adequate notion of the extent of their working. Take this little item which I have clipped from the last number of one of our religious newspapers, describing the payment of the debt of a Congregational church in a western city:

"'The pleasantest feature of the occasion was the remarkably hearty and substantial expressions of interest on the part of the other denominations. They closed their churches Sabbath evening, and some of them in the morning also; and the several pastors were to be seen moving among the congregation, soliciting subscriptions from their own people. Monday evening, when it seemed as if the ability of the audience had been exhausted, and there remained several hundred dollars of the debt yet to be raised, the *Methodist* pastor came to the rescue. By a wise plan, which he pressed with great skill, he raised the entire amount amid great hand-clapping, and declared that, next to the pastor, he was the happiest man in the house.'

"That sounds like an echo from New Albion, does it not? But it is not necessary for me to dwell upon facts that fall under your eyes in all the papers. Let me speak of a matter more remote, but not less notable.

"It is well known to many of you that the sectarianism which we are organized to fight is making its worst ravages on our western frontiers. The strife of the sects for the occupancy of every new settlement is the scandal of Christianity. Every man knows this who has traveled in the West and found in the small towns, on an average, one church for every hundred inhabitants. From this afflicted region I have had letters not a few, rejoicing that this movement had begun at the East, and praying for the time when its tidal wave should begin to roll across their prairies and up their cañons. From a shrewd observer, who knows that western field thoroughly, and who is in the deepest sympathy with the Home Missionary work, comes a letter, from which I will read you a few sentences :

"'The real trouble now is with the intermediate agents of our churches. I mean the presiding elders, the synodical missionaries, and the district superintendents of missionary work. So long as our societies will appoint to such places men whose only qualification is business push — men of about the caliber of a good book-agent, men who could push a cyclopedia in a State — so long there will be confusion enough. I could tell of some in this great work that are perfectly unscrupulous. Our societies must be made to see that they *must* get men who will look at the work broadly, and build with eternity, not quarterly reports, in view. The policy of each missionary society should be expressed, not implied; and agents should be held to account for pushing in where not needed.'

"This extract shows that the responsibility for the state of things existing at the West belongs largely at the East. The power behind this pushing propagandism has its head-quarters in Boston and New York. If you want to get at it, you can easily reach it. But let me give you another bit of the same letter. Speaking of the results of this sectarian scramble at the West, the writer says:

"'I am quite sure it is very seriously affecting the character of our ministry. Who but a mean-spirited man will consent to be one of five in a town of five hundred people? Then, is it not near to the sin against the Holy Ghost thus to misuse the gifts of the Spirit? What wonder ministers are scarce, when they are employed in this way, four or five crowded into a place where there is need of but one, and set in antagonism and rivalry, with no chance to develop any spiritual power? And all the while the world is full of heathenism! Really, this is the most serious phase of the question. A gift of the Spirit, a man furnished by the Spirit for the ministry, is a gift infinitely more precious than the money to feed him; and the misuse of such an one, or the misapplication of the gift, comes nearer to malfeasance than any misuse of funds.'

"This man writes out of his heart, you see. And he writes not unadvisedly. No man in the West is better qualified to judge. And I beg you to note what he says respecting the effect of sectarianism on the character of ministers. I confess that this was to me a flash of revelation. But who can question the truth of it? What kind of a Christian is the man likely to become whose character is developed in these denominational bear-fights? What kind of a Christian is the man who is ready to rush into them? I tell you, high-minded young men will not do it. And many a young man who would gladly give his life to pioneer work on the frontiers, turns back when he sees into what sort of scrimmage he is pretty sure to be driven.

"But I am only showing you the evils of this denominational strife. Of these you hardly needed to be told, though my correspondent may have thrown new light on their deformity. What I began to tell you was the good news that the Christian League has been heard of on the frontiers, and that its good seed is beginning to find lodgment in a soil where it ought to bring forth a hundred fold. We have heard some cheerful tidings here to-day, but none to me so significant as this which I read you from the representative of one of our Home Mission boards in the far West. He tells of a conference, lasting all day, between the Home Missionary representatives of four leading denominations,— four men who have the oversight of two or three Territories. He says that they came to this conference with the Christian League in their minds, and this is his report of what came of it:

"'We did not organize; had no chairman or secretary, and passed no votes, but simply looked one another in the face, and tried to look the facts of the field in the face. We took up the case of each place — went from ——, on the ——, to ——, covering the whole field. We did not realize my *highest* ideal of such a meeting, which would be the consulting entirely as though we were of one denomination; but I believe it was a long step in the right direction. We have arranged not to go into a town where another denomination is at work, when there is any chance for misunderstanding, without consulting with the representatives of the church in that town, or with the superintendent of mission work. We have promised one another not to take advantage of temporary bad luck in getting ministers. We have arranged to exchange fields and properties, as far as possible, when it becomes evident that the best interests of the cause demand it. I have, for instance, given up our church at —— to the ——ists, as the people are nearly all of that faith and ask for a ——ist minister. The ——ists have given up a field to me. The ——ans promise not to enter a field where we have a church, though pressed by some to do so. We have arranged for another meeting in six months.'

"Now, I say that's the best report we have had to-day. It makes me feel more like shouting hallelujah! than anything I've heard for many a day. And if this were *my* meeting-house, and were not the meeting-house of a very staid and undemonstrative body of disciples (laughter), I should call for three cheers for those grand fellows out West who have got the denominational devil fairly under, and who have set out to treat one another, in their mission work, like Christian gentlemen!"

As Mr. Franklin went down from the platform, amid a tempest of hand-clapping, the organ and the choir burst forth with the doxology, in which the congregation joined, and the convention went out in a blaze of enthusiasm.

Mr. Strong and his English friend walked quietly away to their lodgings. The first to speak, when they were out of the hubbub, was Mr. Thornton:

"Doesn't your friend need a vacation?"

"Franklin?"

"The same."

"He does, indeed. I have been urging him to go abroad."

"He must go. He shall go. I want him to help me organize a Christian League Club in Manchester. That is the place to begin."

"Do you think it would work on your side the water?"

"Why shouldn't it? It might need some modifications. But it proposes nothing more than the Christianizing of our churches."

"And nothing less, you might add."

"And nothing less! It is a great thing to undertake, but he would be a faithless Christian who should doubt whether it could come to pass."

A POSTSCRIPT.

From The Century Magazine for September, 1883.

THANK you, Mr. Editor, for giving me just the chance I want to grind my own little hatchet. Your types, far better than my hectograph, will multiply the answer that I ought to make to the many who are writing me kind and curious letters about " The Christian League of Connecticut." Mr. Franklin mentioned, at the last convention, the large correspondence which had grown out of his connection with the League as its secretary; and upon me, as its historian, an almost equal burden has been thrown. Some of the inquirers write to headquarters, as they should; but letters directed to the League at Hartford are sometimes forwarded to me. A few of my English correspondents seem to be puzzled by the geography, but that is nothing strange for Englishmen. If Mr. Franklin should visit England, as I hope he may, he will undoubtedly prepare a large map, after the manner of the missionary secretaries, showing the location of the principal League

Clubs, and indicating with spots of some bright color the towns in which churches have been consolidated. I trust that my English friends will avail themselves of the opportunity of hearing Mr. Franklin's lecture, if for no other purpose, that they may obtain a little information about American geography.

The grateful and appreciative words that have come to me from all quarters give me far greater honor than belongs to me. In making the record that I have made of this beneficent movement, I have only done my duty. The praise is due to those—and they are many, nor do they all live in Connecticut—in whose minds and hearts this impulse toward coöperation in Christian work lives and grows from year to year. It is plain that a destructive analysis has done its worst upon the Church, and that we have reached a period of reconstruction and synthesis. The fragments of the great denominations steadily gravitate together; the Presbyterians, North and South, are beginning to talk in their assemblies about coming together, and disunion can never survive discussion. No man can give a Christian reason for opposing reunion; every reason against it is drawn from selfish considerations or hateful passions which Christian men cannot long justify themselves in cherishing. When the Presbyterians come together, the Methodists and the Baptists cannot afford to stay apart, and we shall presently see the centripetal forces acting as vigorously as the centrifugal forces have been acting for a century or two. All this is in the air. He who cannot discern it is dull-witted indeed. I have only reported the movements of the *Zeitgeist*.

Mr. Franklin made a few quotations from his letters. Let me give an extract or two from mine, to indicate the depth of the feeling on this subject, and the social and ecclesiastical conditions out of which this feeling springs. A minister of the Methodist Episcopal Church in New England writes to me as follows:

"You see from my address where I am. Here are five churches and only eight hundred people in the entire township. The —— church has no regular preaching. The other churches are in good order as to buildings and parsonages. The Methodists are said to have the largest congregations. At my first service, last Sunday, there were eighty-six. The salaries are three hundred and fifty or four hundred dollars and rent, save that the —— clergyman has to pay his rent from his salary of four hundred dollars. * * * It seems to me that as long as such churches can get men to be pastors they will stick to their narrow denominational ideas and have different churches. But I do not think that God has called me into the ministry for any such purpose. One of the clergymen said he had been very happy here for ten years, and thought I should be. I cannot be, unless I can bring about some union of these churches. With the call for men to heathen lands and the West, how can I be happy here? * * * This much is settled. I cannot give my life to the preservation of mere denominational lines. What can I do in the way of the Christian League? Have you those articles in pamphlet form? If I could put one in every family here, and call a meeting in the large, beautiful town hall!"

The good man in his perplexity sees a glimmer of light in the West; but there is reason to fear that his flight thither would prove to be only a translation from a Yankee frying-pan to a prairie fire, as the following extracts will show. The writer of the letter from which they are taken is a Congregational minister in the far West—a man with the most ample knowledge of all that region, and with a grasp of mind and a temper of soul that speak for themselves:

"I am convinced that if the policy of our missionary societies could be this, to have fewer churches and better, to withdraw from competition in many a hopeless field, that we may do the right thing where the way is open and the need great, we should do a much better work than we do. Only last week I was told by Rev. —— ——, who has long known Kansas, that he knew of fifty places in which the Congregationalists and Presbyterians should unite. If that could be done so that there would be twenty-five less Congregational churches and twenty-five less Presbyterian, there would be (1) a saving of fifteen thousand dollars missionary money; (2) a saving of an indefinite amount for church buildings; (3) the release of fifty men to preach the Gospel in other places; (4) fifty fields that would be an attraction to men of spirit, in the place of fifty fields that no one but a mendicant would think of taking.

"*I am not at all surprised at the scarcity of ministers.* The policy of our home missionary societies tends to keep men from the ministry. We have a dead and dreary level of little churches that offer no inviting field for young men. It is easy to say that any young man fit for the ministry ought to be ready to enter the smallest field, that he ought to have the spiritual efficiency to make his small field a large one. I have said this myself. It is the true thing to say. But if the field is small, not because of the wickedness of sinners, but because of the folly of saints and the mistakes of the home missionary authorities, the case becomes hopeless. We must expect to begin small in new places; the trouble is that our fields remain small, and must remain so while this mistaken policy continues. If a young man is asked to endure hardships for Christ's sake, by all means let us not take the courage out of him by false pity; but if it turns out that the call for self-sacrifice is not for Christ at all, but for *our Church*, we need not wonder if the truest consecration comes to be a forgotten grace, and that the best men cannot be found for the ministry."

The writers of these letters—and I have many like them—are not theorists; they are men who stand in the midst of this sectarian confusion, and who are doing their best to bring a little order out of its tumult, and to mix a little sweetness with its bitter waters. Such voices have a right to be heard, and they will be heard. The men who have the ordering of the work of our home missionary societies must attend to these mischiefs at once. Some of them, as I happen to know, are heartily disposed to do so; others, I fear, are ready to wink at any amount of "scrouging" if it do but inure to the benefit of their respective sects.

I will add but one word more, that the scarcity of ministers, so much complained of, is due, as my Western correspondent shows, to the spirit of schism, perhaps quite as much as to any other cause. There would be no lack of ministers, even numerically, if the churches that have no right to exist were blotted out. And if that were done, we should soon report a great gain not only in the number, but also in the quality of the men seeking the ministry.

www.ingramcontent.com/pod-product-compliance
Lightning Source LLC
Chambersburg PA
CBHW020843160426
43192CB00007B/767